Praise for *Spiritu~~~~*

Hosea 4:6 says, "My people are destr~ ~~~~~~~~~~~ nd Eddie Smith share prophetic and practical tru~ ~~ for you and your family. I highly commend this outs~

Dr. Ché Ahn
President, Harvest International Ministries
Senior Pastor, Harvest Rock Church, Pasadena, California

Many things in the world today that are called faddish are a fetish. God has opened the eyes of Eddie and Alice Smith's understanding to teach us how to keep these things out of our homes. Open your heart to this book's message and enjoy!

Dr. Kim Daniels
Apostle and Overseer, Spoken Word Ministries, Jacksonville, Florida

Spiritual House Cleaning is a timely message to the Body of Christ, calling us all to a new level of holiness. We have left open spiritual doors to the enemy in our homes, churches and hearts. Alice and Eddie Smith have given us the keys to free ourselves from demonic hindrances that have infiltrated our walk with God.

Francis Frangipane
Author, *The Three Battlegrounds*
Senior Pastor, River of Life Ministries, Cedar Rapids, Iowa

Eddie and Alice Smith have managed to capture with great insight issues that plague many people because of historical and spiritual violations on people's land prior to them purchasing it. I believe this book to be essential in understanding how spiritual powers work and how to combat those forces and ensure God's presence.

John Paul Jackson
Founder, Streams Ministries International

Satan and the forces of evil do everything they can to discourage the Christian—including attempting to invade our homes. This is part of the conflict in the invisible world. We must be aware of and cut off the subtle ways Satan trespasses and attempts to rob us of blessings right where we live. Eddie and Alice Smith point us to the place where we must begin—in our own souls and homes. They show us how to cleanse our attitudes and every physical room where we reside. The Smiths give us a step-by-step guide to taking unlimited authority over demons and reclaiming our homes for the Lord. They show us how to apply the biblical truth that in God's wonderful order, "He who is in you is greater than he who is in the world" (1 John 4:4).

Pat Robertson
Host, The 700 Club
Founder and Chairman, The Christian Broadcasting Network

If we are ignorant of the wiles of the devil, he will surely take advantage of us. With *Spiritual House Cleaning*, Eddie and Alice Smith have exposed his wiles and dealt a severe blow to the kingdom of darkness. This book will help you break satanic bondages and set you free for victory!

C. Peter Wagner
Chancellor, Wagner Leadership Institute
President, Global Harvest Ministries, Colorado Springs, Colorado

SPIRITUAL
HOUSE
CLEANING
WORKBOOK

EDDIE & ALICE SMITH

Regal

From Gospel Light
Ventura, California, U.S.A.

Published by Regal Books
From Gospel Light
Ventura, California, U.S.A.
Printed in the U.S.A.

Smith, Eddie.
Spiritual house cleaning workbook / Eddie and Alice Smith.
p. cm.
ISBN 978-0-8307-4381-0 (trade paper)
1. Spiritual warfare. I. Smith, Alice. II. Title.
BV4509.5.S622 2007
235'.4—dc22
2007008366

Rights for publishing this book in other languages are contracted
by Gospel Light Worldwide, the international nonprofit ministry of
Gospel Light. For additional information,
visit www.gospellightworldwide.org.

Contents

CHAPTER 1

The Need for Spiritual Housecleaning

The Indian sun blazed, raising temperatures to 118 degrees Fahrenheit by midday. People were dying due to the excessive heat. To protect themselves, most would work until about 10:00 A.M., retreat inside until sundown and then return to resume their business and shopping.

Robert, our eldest son, and I (Eddie) were in Karapur, India, to teach at a Christian conference (and, by the grace of God, we managed to survive the heat!). Over 300 Indian Christians joined us there, bearing the intense heat as they rode bicycles, buses and trains—some for days—in order to attend the conference. Once there, they slept on concrete floors, bathed out of buckets and ate food cooked over outdoor fires.

We taught various subjects, but my teaching on spiritual housecleaning had the most far-reaching impact on this idol-worshiping culture. As I spoke about unbiblical heathen practices and cultural traditions, I could see them removing Hindu fetishes (i.e., string bracelets, necklaces and charms that they wore in hopes that a particular god would protect or provide for them) from their bodies and from their pockets and purses.

I gave the altar call. With zeal they brought those forbidden, spiritually defiling items to the altar and discarded them (see Acts 19:18-19). Freedom rang out like church bells in the hearts of those precious people that day! Curses were broken, generational sin was severed and spiritual liberty was released. Some people got healed and others saved. The next day we baptized 67 in a public city pond!

Robert and I left the hotel the day after our conference to catch our plane for the United States. We'd been gone from the hotel for about 30 minutes when we received a phone call telling us that the police had come to the hotel to arrest us—just minutes after we left. God spared us the trouble.

Why did they want to arrest us? Was it because 67 people had trusted Christ? Was it because 67 people had renounced their Hindu faith and been baptized? No. It was because we had taught them that their Hindu worship artifacts were evil, defiled and forbidden by God. The newspapers reported that we had offended and belittled their Hindu gods and that we'd converted 300 of their people. They didn't understand a thing about the true conversion of the 67 who received eternal life, but instead focused on the 300 who disposed of their fetishes.

Wouldn't you agree that if our asking people to divest themselves of these things offended the Hindu priests so much that they sent police to arrest us, it's safe to assume that those things (or, rather, the Hindu "gods" behind them) held some sort of power over them? And that our possessing those kinds of things glorifies devils and grieves the one true God (see Acts 24-29; 1 Corinthians 10:18-22)?

Genesis 35:1-5 gives us a biblical example of this truth:

> And God said unto Jacob, "Arise, go up to Bethel and dwell there; and make there an altar unto God, who appeared unto thee when thou fleddest from the face of Esau thy brother." Then Jacob said unto his household and to all that were with him, "*Put away the strange gods that are among you,* and be clean and change your garments. And let us arise and go up to Bethel; and I will make there an altar unto God, who answered me in the day of my distress, and was with me in the way which I went." And they gave unto Jacob all the strange gods which were in their hand, and all their earrings which were in their ears; and Jacob hid them under the oak which was by Shechem. And they journeyed; *and the terror of God was upon the cities that were round about them, and they did not pursue after the sons of Jacob* (KJ21, emphasis added).

After Jacob and his family got rid of their objects of idolatry, God honored them. His presence went with them and put terror in the hearts of the people around them—people who might otherwise have attacked them. Today, the same power and favor of God is available to us, whether in India, America, Antarctica or anywhere else in the world! Time and again, for nearly 40 years, our experiences with spiritual housecleaning have shown this to be true.

Where Did We Get the Idea for Spiritual Housecleaning?

As itinerant evangelists in the 1970s, we traveled hundreds of thousands of miles, living in a motor home that we lovingly called our piece of "wheel estate." In fact, over the course of that time, we owned seven such vehicles before we stopped traveling! We ministered all over America, conducting evangelistic crusades in churches and football stadiums. We were blessed to see thousands of people come to Christ.

During those early years of our ministry, we did a great deal of personal counseling. Traveling as we did from town to town, we began to recognize spiritual patterns. Regardless of whether we were in a city, in suburbs or in small rural towns we noticed similar things happening in the spiritual realm.

In the late '60s and early '70s, very few books had been written about spiritual warfare or deliverance. *Pigs in the Parlor,* written by our friend the late Frank Hammond, was one of the first. Hollywood's burgeoning fascination with the demonic expressed itself in films like *Rosemary's Baby, Poltergeist* and *The Exorcist,* to name a few. Added to that was the massive influx of immigrants to the United States, arriving with their family gods and religious cultural practices (many ready to build their temples and mosques right in our neighborhoods). Our land quickly became defiled. Don't misunderstand—America had her own demons. But our *Leave It to Beaver* days were over, and demonic manifestations exploded in this nation.

We encountered our first case of a demonized person in a large Baptist church in South Texas. Frankly, we were stunned to witness a "respected churchgoing woman" lying on the floor of her pastor's office, hissing and writhing like a snake, speaking with an unearthly male-sounding voice. From that moment, we were completely convinced that Satan was more than an evil idea or philosophy. He and his minions were real spiritual beings—like people without bodies—who had an intense desire to inhabit a human body to fulfill their lusts and desires and advance Satan's kingdom (see Matthew 12:25-26,43-45).

Soon we were routinely counseling demonized people, leading them through deliverance from the demons that plagued them, many of them from birth. At the same time, we encountered people—godly people, believable people—who were experiencing poltergeists (mischievous demons who move objects), ghosts (demons masquerading as the deceased), and other troubling spiritual phenomenon. Children were the most easily harassed by demons. They suffered from insomnia, nightmares and more.[1]

As our experience grew, so did our understanding. We discovered that the demons that plagued people were in some cases strengthened by unholy possessions—defiled, forbidden objects that dishonored Christ (see Hosea 4:10-13; 1 Corinthians 10:18-22). Almost weekly we saw people who, upon discarding such possessions, experienced freedom from demonic manifestations.

In Acts 19, we see how Ephesian believers destroyed their occultic material when they saw the power of God at work through Paul. In that day, Ephesus was known as a witchcraft capital of the Roman world. It was a city famed for its written collections of occultic spells and for the practitioners who used them. Paul shook the city up when he came preaching the name of Jesus in the power of the Holy Spirit. Through signs, wonders and deliverances, many believed. But it took a demonic attack on the seven sons of Sceva to show the Ephesian Christians that they needed to shut every door to evil activity in their lives (see Acts 19:11–16). When this happened, those believers got the message: Jesus is the highest power in the universe! They then burned their books of the occult and of witchcraft and confessed their sins publicly. What happened next? "The word of God grew mightily and prevailed!" (Acts 19:17-20).

What Personal Experiences Did We Have with Spiritual Housecleaning?

One night in the early '70s, during a revival meeting in a Southern state, there was a gathering at the pastor's home. One of the ladies in the group caught our attention. We both discerned a spiritual defilement about her. Jane (not her real name) was the music minister's wife, and her husband was out of town during our week of revival services. Before the week was over, we found ourselves counseling with her concerning her sexual involvement with one of the teenage boys in the church. (Yes, she was sexually active with one of the church's own teens!)

At one point we asked Jane about her salvation. She said she was saved one night while driving her truck. This young pretty woman said that a voice whispered in her left ear, "Give me your life."

And she said, "Lord, I *do* give you my life."

We probed, "And to whom were you speaking?"

She said, "What do you mean, 'to whom'? I was speaking to God."

"How did you know it was God?"

"You mean it might have been a demon spirit?"

"God speaks in the heart."

It was then that she realized that from the moment she made this agreement, her life began a downhill slide. (If you ask God for a fish, He won't give you a serpent, but a devil certainly would.) In Matthew 7:17-20, Jesus said that the "fruits"—people's actions and character—show whether the source of that fruit is good and from God or bad and not from God. This woman's decision produced the bad fruit of greater and greater oppression and sin in her life. This showed that she had unwittingly committed her life to demons.

The bottom line? She was born again and delivered that week. All the issues came out for the necessary parties to bring correction.

Two weeks later her husband called to tell us she was suffering terribly from the temptation to rekindle the relationship with the boy. Through phone counseling, we discovered that she had a blouse and a necklace that the young man had given her as gifts. Those items, we explained, were physical representations of their sin. They strengthened the "soul tie" (a spiritual attachment between people brought about through evil actions or unholy covenants between them). It wasn't until she destroyed them that she was finally freed. People can develop godly soul ties, like Jonathan and David (see 1 Samuel 18:1) or ungodly soul ties, like Samson and Delilah (see Judges 16:4-19).

Because we were traveling evangelists, we had far more experiences and encounters than we would have had were we pastors in one locale.

One night in a tiny Tennessee church, we found ourselves in a pastor's study, trying to help a delinquent teenage girl. When her unwed teenage mother gave birth to her, that young mother's parents tried to cover their daughter's sin. They sent their daughter away until she gave birth. During that time, they moved to another city and didn't tell extended family members about the pregnancy or the birth.

When the girl to whom we were ministering was born, they adopted her and never disclosed to her that she was their granddaughter, *not* their daughter. The girl was taught and believed that her actual mother was really her older sister, until one of her cousins discovered the deception and told the girl about it. From that point she became depressed, suspicious and severely troubled.

Her mother and father (actually grandmother and grandfather) brought her to us for counseling. When they told us how they had lied to her, we insisted that they tell their granddaughter the truth. No matter how painful it would be, we knew that she could not build a healthy life on lies. That night they finally disclosed to her that she was their granddaughter and that her "sister" was actually her mother. She was devastated, but in her heart she had known for some time that something didn't seem right. She had been lied to all her life, and it affected her very identity.

We ministered deliverance to her, but after an hour or so we hit the proverbial brick wall. Stymied, we prayed for God to reveal what our problem was. Why were we impotent against the spirits that bound her?

Then we noticed something in a lower bookshelf. The pastor's bottom bookshelf contained a copy of Anton Levy's *Satanic Bible,* along with several other occult handbooks. We asked the pastor why he had them. He said he had bought them for research.

We explained to him that they were compromising the young lady's deliverance. We stopped our session, took the books outside to a trash-burning bin and set fire to them. It was almost impossible to get them lit, but after we did, the most amazing thing happened (since then we've seen this many times and hear about it often): No matter which side of the bin we chose to stand on, regardless of the direction of the slight breeze that night, the flames licked out at us. When we moved away from the bin, they licked farther, trying to reach us. It was almost as if the flames had minds of their own. Once the books were finally destroyed, this young lady was completely set free by the Lord.

Why Did We Write the First Book?

In the 1980s, I (Eddie) took a church pastoral staff job, and we bought a house and settled down. Alice became an award-winning realtor. During the next 11 years, we served a local church congregation in Houston, Texas.

It wasn't long before we began to encounter similar experiences with the demonic among our members, and then other churches began to send us people who needed counseling involving the supernatural, demons and the rest. One night we were facilitating the deliverance of a dear lady in northwest Houston. To make an extremely long story short, we and another pastor from our church were challenging the demons that were tormenting the lady when we asked, "What gives you the right to stay in her?"

With that, the lady's arm involuntarily moved above her head and pointed to a bookshelf with a sliding door. We opened the door and discovered a "Christian" book about demons. "This?" we asked.

The lady's face twisted into a sarcastic sneer, and the demon (speaking through her) said devilishly, "Yes."

Without a thought, I ripped the book into shreds before her. As I did, the demons shrieked and left her. She was freed. (We suggest that you validate the fruit of an author's work—possibly by Googling their name on the Internet and doing a little research—to make sure that what you are reading isn't lies and deception.)

We (our pastoral team) learned to minister to people using ministry teams of three to five people. Soon we had developed a system we called Ministry Team Training to teach our church members how to minister in teams. Before long, hundreds of people from churches across the South were coming to our church to be trained at those training events. The course further developed as the experience of our team grew. Soon we had established multiple levels of training.

Shortly after leaving the church to do the work we now do—writing and teaching at conferences around the world—we wrote the book

Spiritual House Cleaning, which presents some of our experiences and explains some of our conclusions. It provides answers to difficult questions that many people wanted answered but didn't know who to ask.

In it, we presented a biblical basis for believing that physical things can represent spiritual things and can either strengthen or weaken spiritual power—God's or Satan's.

Using the story of Achan's sin in Joshua, chapter seven, we explained how one person's sin of possessing God-forbidden things can open the door to the demonic and spiritually cripple that person, their family and even their church. Scripture says that when one member of the Body suffers, the whole Body suffers (see 1 Corinthians 12:26)!

To our amazement (and perhaps our publisher's!), *Spiritual House Cleaning* became an overnight bestseller. In fact, it was number 2 on the top 100 Christian books list for several months that year. Letters began pouring in from around the world, reporting stories and experiences that people from various cultures and languages were having that related to what we had written. Many had found victory as a result of reading our book, taking it to heart and applying the biblical principles we prescribed.

In this follow-up to our original book, we share some of their stories with you. Why? To help you see even more clearly why living a life of purity and victory depends partly upon our forsaking things that dishonor Christ and His kingdom. And to help you understand that evil uses the same mode of operation wherever it exists around the world. Evil is neither creative nor complex. In fact, it's quite predictable.

Fasten your seatbelt. Some of these stories will amaze you. But we aren't the least bit interested in your entertainment. We pray that you'll receive new revelation of the strategies of the enemy so that you can live free and set others free. Scripture clearly teaches that evil will become more wicked and righteousness will shine more brightly until the coming of our Lord for His Church (see Isaiah 60:1-3; Daniel 12:3; Matthew 13:24-43; 2 Timothy 3:13). Let's prepare for the worst and the best that's to come.

Note

1. To learn more about deliverance, see Alice Smith, *Delivering the Captives* (Grand Rapids, MI: Bethany House, 2003), available at www.prayerbookstore.com.

Chapter 2

Home-Front Stories of Spiritual Housecleaning

In America today, home improvement TV shows reveal how consumers collectively spend millions each year on everything from bathrooms to blinds, landscaping to light fixtures, all in attempts to create the perfect look and atmosphere for their homes. Sadly, much of the interior décor Christians buy to create this "perfect look" in their homes includes crystal pyramids, Buddhist picture plaques, gold-leaf dragon coffee tables, sphinx heads and religious icons from around the world. But a new coat of paint for your home has far less to do with a home's true environment than do the elements inside and around it. How is the spiritual environment inside your home? Is your home illuminated by the light of Christ or dimmed by spiritual darkness? Is it a place of peace or panic? Do you run *to your home* as a refuge or run *from your home* because of the inexplicable oppression you feel within it?

In this chapter we share the stories of those who *cleaned house* on a deeply spiritual (and profoundly practical) level. We look at why different residents experienced nightmares and insomnia, unemployment and illness, ghostly appearances and bizarre manifestations that provoked fear and frustration in their lives. We reveal how various objects and activities opened the door to the demonic forces behind those things. These stories examine what lay at the root of each experience, thus exposing the enemy's tactics for taking ground in a home. We also explore more Scripture related to this topic and give you tools for taking action in your own home.

Sensations, Smells and Sleepless Nights

Spiritual housecleaning can change a home's physical environment. Sue White tells the following story about how this affected her home:

This story takes place back in the early 1990s when writing books was just a glint in Eddie's and Alice's eyes. Alice had helped us find a foreclosed home in Houston, Texas, in a nice neighborhood just across the road from our children's school and a short drive from our church.

Things couldn't have been better until we began to notice some strange things happening in our home. There was a strange smell that seemed to drift out of the air conditioning vent in our master bedroom, and the temperature in Robin's, our oldest daughter's, bedroom was considerably colder than the other rooms in the house. We tried to explain away these things as "normal"—a mouse or bird could somehow have gotten access to our attic and died up there, giving off a putrid odor—but on a regular, ongoing basis? Aren't there always rooms in a house that have uneven airflow, creating cold spots? Our thinking was just to close the air-vent down a bit and warm the room up a few degrees—right? Well, not so in this case.

Eddie was the associate pastor at our church; Alice was an awesome Bible teacher and intercessor. We learned about deliverance, spiritual mapping and spiritual housecleaning from their teachings. It amazed us to learn that spiritual entities could take residence in people, inanimate objects and buildings. By now, our teenage daughter was also experiencing difficulty sleeping and would awake with nightmares. We felt it was worth checking into the possibility that our house had some unwanted "guests" in residence, so I called Eddie to discuss my suspicions and scheduled him to come pray through our home.

Eddie arrived at the scheduled time and began walking through our home. He didn't immediately indicate his feelings, but patiently listened as I explained the unusual things that were happening. He then explained the process as he prayed through each room, pointing out any defilement and ending by praying a blessing over our home and family. It was amazing what began to unfold!

In the dining room near the front entrance, Eddie received a revelation that there was something "dark" in there. He told us that he never "saw" demons but that he could sometimes sense their presence. He was given a word of knowledge that the previous owner's son played Dungeons and Dragons in the dining room with his friends, and that several spirits were given permission to abide there through playing that game. Eddie rebuked the evil spirits and sent them packing! As a follow-up to Eddie's visit I interviewed some of my neighbors who knew the previous owners of our home, and they confirmed that the teenage son played D&D in that room during most of his waking hours.

We progressed to the master bedroom where the putrid odor—the smell of something dead—would come in. The strange thing was that you could never smell it outside of that room. Eddie rebuked whatever was causing the odor and indicated they no longer had permission to invade our home. From that day forward we never had that smell in our bedroom.

Finally we arrived at our daughter's bedroom. Did I mention that my husband was an air-conditioning technician and had done all of the normal tricks to the thermostat, air vents and a/c unit in an attempt to balance the temperature in this room? As Eddie prayed in this room, he began to focus on the closet. He said, "Sue, there's something right in this spot that seems to be causing the problem."

The doors of the closet were closed, so he could not see any of its contents. We opened the doors and began to look through the items near the area he pointed out. A jewelry box sat on a shelf at this spot. We removed the box and began going through its contents. There were a number of pieces of costume jewelry and trinkets that Robin had collected. One necklace seemed to draw Eddie's attention. It had a crystal-looking pendant with the image of a Chinese pagoda etched into it.[1] This had sentimental value attached to it, in that my father had bought this for my mother years ago during a visit to San Francisco. My mother thought it would be nice for Robin to have a remembrance of her grandfather. Eddie felt strongly that this was the item that was causing the disturbance. He suggested that since it had sentimental value we first try moving the necklace out to the garage to see if anything changed in the bedroom. If things improved, then a decision would have to be made as to what to do about it.

Within hours the temperature began to change in that room, and in the nights that followed, our daughter no longer was plagued with nightmares. After praying about it as a family, we decided to throw the necklace in the trash rather than give it back to my mother. There was no sense shifting our problems to another location and allowing the demonic spirits to plague someone else.

We were finally rid of the foul spirits that had interrupted our home. Eddie's prayer of blessing was wonderful, and our subsequent visitors always remarked at how restful their visits were at our home. Thank you, Eddie and Alice, for opening our eyes to the power of prayer and the need for spiritual housecleaning!

What were the Whites' first indicators that something wasn't right in their home?

_____

_____

_____

_____

_____

What was their first response to what they experienced?

_____

_____

_____

_____

When those practical steps failed to solve the problems, what was their next course of action?

_____

_____

_____

_____

_____

Read Mark 5:1-13. Give a summary of this story. What did the demons plead with Jesus to do with them, and where did He send them?

_____

_____

_____

_____

_____

_____

_____

_____

What does this say to you about demons possessing/inhabiting something other than a human being?

_____

_____

_____

_____

_____

_____

_____

_____

Have you experienced anything that you think might be a physical manifestation of demonic spirits in your home? If so, describe what you've experienced.

_____

_____

_____

_____

_____

_____

_____

_____

If so, what steps have you taken to rid your home of the problem, and what have been the results?

_____

_____

_____

_____

_____

_____

_____

_____

If you haven't addressed the problem yet, what, based on reading Sue's story, will you do *today* to start the spiritual housecleaning process? List the steps you will take.

_____

_____

_____

_____

_____

_____

_____

Ungodly Clutter

In the following story, I (Alice) explain how one couple made a clean sweep of religious icons and idols inside their home. After we identified the problems and gave the couple instructions on what to do, within weeks, their health, finances and circumstances completely changed.

> I was in our office when a call came in from a woman who lives in our city. She and her husband had read our book *Spiritual House Cleaning* and felt they needed a lot of help. (Be assured, I would never get anything done if I took all the calls that I receive each day, but I knew the Holy Spirit wanted me to answer this one.)

She said, "My husband, Calvin, and I are both sick. We are one week away from our house going into foreclosure, and we have a completely renovated townhouse that we've not been able to rent for three years. We are dealing with two unjust lawsuits, no work is coming in, and we are $50,000 behind in taxes. We read your book, but there are so many things wrong with our home, we don't know what to do. Can you help us?"

"Where do you live?" I asked.

"Just off the freeway," was her reply.

I sensed the Lord say that I was to take a team of women to their house and pray, so we set the appointment. I called my weekly prayer team and they agreed to join me at Calvin and Sandi's house for our regular Wednesday morning prayer time.

The house was a typical Houston home with a large yard filled with many old oak trees, all trailing Spanish moss. The yards in the neighborhood were nicely manicured for established homes, but our new friends' home was a different story. They too would have admitted that the front yard and driveway looked as if a perpetual garage sale had been going on. There were flatbed trailers filled with street lamps, barbecue equipment and other miscellaneous things. But the front of their house was only a preview of what was inside.

Upon our entering the house, Calvin and Sandi graciously introduced themselves to each of us, and we visited for a few minutes. It wasn't hard to see why they were so overwhelmed. There was clutter and chaos from corner to corner.

Calvin and Sandi began to tell us how the Worshipful Master of the Masonic Lodge (located two blocks away) had built the home. Many of the meetings for the Masons had been held in their home while waiting for the lodge to be built. The wife had named the middle room "the devil's den" because it was there she would smoke her cigarettes and drink her wine. All the neighbors knew about her room. But the disturbing part is that when the home was sold to the second family, the teenage son's room was the middle bedroom. He was a very troubled teen whom friends said "dedicated the house to the devil," and he was obsessed with Marilyn Manson's music. Calvin and Sandi had never heard of spiritual housecleaning before reading our book, but they knew something was very wrong with their home.

After a time of prayer, we moved from room to room to see what the Lord might be saying. Every room had crucifixes (representations of Jesus hanging *dead* on the cross). Some were in drawers, some were visible and some were in jewelry boxes. I asked Sandi about this, and she told me that her background was Catholic, even though she was now born again and a faithful member of a wonderful church. Her mother, a strict adherent to praying to Mary, had continued to give her pictures of Mary and crucifixes all different one from the other. Out of respect, she had kept them all.

If you have a Catholic background, please prayerfully consider the following. The crucifix and the cross are different images. The cross is empty—Jesus isn't there. However, the crucifix has Jesus still hanging there. The crucifix, in Satan's mind, is a "photograph" of his finest hour. He succeeded in killing Jesus. Whether carved in wood, chiseled in stone, painted in oils or molded in bronze, a crucifix presents a dead, helpless God, which may provoke many people to pity, but few to saving faith. Many Catholic paintings and symbols present Christ as weak, emaciated, sickly or dead—incapable of helping Himself or others.

We are certainly grateful for Christ's sacrifice on the cross. Through the death of Jesus, we have salvation from our sins. He died in our stead. But the cross is not to be seen as a tragedy. To believers, it is a victory! The crucifixion isn't the highpoint of the gospel. The empty cross and the open tomb are!

If you question this, reread the sermons in the New Testament. The apostles preached, "Jesus of Nazareth . . . you have taken by lawless hands, have crucified and put to death. This Jesus God has raised up, of which we are all witnesses" (Acts 2:23,24,32). Stop right now and read Acts 2:23-36; 3:15; 4:10; 5:30-31; 10:39-41; 13:28-37 and 17:30-32. It is true! The gospel message that the apostles preached and for which they died contains three times as much about His resurrection as His crucifixion! The cross and the tomb are empty! Our message to the world is, "Jesus is alive!"

Perhaps not surprisingly, cultures that have adhered to the crucifix, with its dead, helpless Jesus, have been some of the hardest to reach with the gospel. But perhaps Paul's statement in 1 Corinthians 15:14 gives us insight: "And if Christ has not been raised, our preaching is useless and so is your faith" (*NIV*). Millions of people worldwide are receiving a revelation of this truth—the power of the gospel is in the risen Savior!

Don't overlook religious paraphernalia when considering your possessions. We have seen great freedom come to those who parted with religious icons for the sake of their risen and ascended Lord. Don't let your undue attachment to religious images, whether because you or your past relatives valued them, hinder your Christian walk.

It's one thing *to give things to God* in order that we might live for Him, but it's another thing, as the rich young ruler learned, *to give up things for God* in order that we might be liberated from the grip of this world. Struggling with this issue? Just remember: "When He, the Spirit of truth, has come, He will guide you into all truth; for He will not speak on His own authority, but whatever He hears He will speak; and He will tell you things to come" (John 16:13).

Let's continue Calvin and Sandi's story.

We found Masonic emblems, scores of crucifixes, coffee cups with zodiac symbols on them and questionable movies and pictures. Just walking through the cluttered house was a challenge for my team; but as we prayed and broke contracts along the way, especially in the second bedroom, the Spirit of God was more and more obviously present with us. One of our prayer-team ladies felt led to pray for Calvin and Sandi's physical healing, and God showed up powerfully—standing in the kitchen, both Calvin and Sandi almost collapsed into our arms! I instructed them to clean their home one room at a time and to pray over each room, dedicating it to the Lord and His glory. I reminded them of the steps outlined in our book. Calvin and Sandi appeared excited and motivated.

Two weeks later I called Sandi. "How's it going?" praying that she had taken my advice.

"Oh, my goodness, you won't believe it, Alice! We have thrown away so much stuff that our neighbors continue to come to the door and ask if we are moving. Both of the lawsuits that were against us have been supernaturally dismissed and one of our clients has paid his bill of over $1,000. Our house won't go into foreclosure, because God has provided the three months of back payments that were due. And yesterday morning, three people called wanting to rent our townhouse. The biggest shock was that two of the potential renters raced to our door to try to get the contract first. Our teenage daughter is so excited about our spiritual housecleaning that instead of visiting with her friends, she decided to stay home just to help us. We have felt lighter and lighter with every bag full of trash and all the dishonorable things we've thrown out. We still have a lot to do, but after the first week of cleaning, my business phone began to ring again. And Calvin's knee is so much better. Call me back in a couple more weeks, once we're finished."

A week later I got a surprise call from Sandi. "You know our back taxes? Well, I called the IRS and they have agreed to work out a payment plan that we can handle. Before now they were so mean and unhelpful, all I could do was cry in discouragement."

One month later I called Sandi. With incredible excitement Sandi said, "Our house is so clean. I found dozens of crucifixes and unbelievable junk that we didn't even realize we had kept from our 'ungodly days.' We're sleeping soundly now and our aches and pains are very few. It's remarkable the miracles we have experienced, and it is all from reading your book *Spiritual House Cleaning*."

"But I must tell you about the final night," Sandi continued. "I was about to fall asleep, when I heard the Holy Spirit say to me, 'Sandi, you missed a crucifix. It's caught in the back of your jewelry box.' I sat up in the bed, amazed. I realized that it had been years since I had heard the voice of the Holy Spirit so clearly. I got up and walked over to my standing jewelry case. Bending over,

I pulled each drawer out to peer into the back where the crucifix might have been caught. To my surprise, there it was, just as the Lord had said. I reached in and pulled out a crucifix necklace that had been snagged on the felt-lined back wall of the case. This crucifix, a European version, was particularly gory, as Jesus looked so emaciated and defeated. I repented to the Lord, threw it away and broke all contracts with death that had for so long filled our home. I slept like a baby that night. We are free, free, free!"

It's been four years since all this happened, but recently I called Calvin to ask him to do some carpentry work for us. I asked, "How are you guys doing?"

Calvin answered, "We're absolutely great! I can't stay on top of all the business that is coming in, and in fact I can't get to the work you want done for another two weeks. And the same is true for Sandi. We are almost completely debt-free, except for the taxes, but that is coming along well, too. We are healthy, our home is clean, and we are truly grateful for the investment you made in writing *Spiritual House Cleaning*. It saved our lives."

Whew! What a huge weight was lifted from Sandi's and Calvin's shoulders! It must have been like being born again, *again*! Have you ever felt as if you were suffocating under a heap of junk or entangled in a web of financial worries with no idea how to escape?

Read Proverbs 22:4 and 1 Peter 5:5. What are these verses about?

_____

_____

_____

_____

_____

_____

_____

_____

_____

_____

What steps did Calvin and Sandi take *after* they received help from us?

_____

_____

_____

_____

_____

_____

_____

Humility is a vital key if you are to receive help from the Holy Spirit and others. Perhaps you've cried out to God for help before but have been reluctant to let go of your possessions and your *pride* as well. If so and if you're now willing to change, take a moment and humble yourself before God and repent for being stubborn. Only as we submit to Him and humble ourselves before others will we be able to receive the help we need to get truly free from spiritual bondage. Perhaps your house is not as bad as Calvin and Sandi's, but even the tidiest home can collect spiritual clutter. Something as simple as a teacup, a toy, a piece of jewelry or a DVD can have significant impact on an otherwise spiritually clean home.

Do you have any rosaries (refer to *Spiritual House Cleaning*), crucifixes, pictures or images of Mary that distract from focusing on Jesus and His victory for you at His resurrection? Do you have any statues of Buddha, Shiva or any other false god; Tarot cards; books related to Buddhism, Hinduism, Scientology, Jehovah's Witnesses, New Age, Freemasonry, Mormonism, witchcraft; or other occult objects in your home? If so, list them below. Which of these things have you located in your home? What spiritual housecleaning steps will you take regarding them?

_____

_____

_____

_____

_____

_____

_____

Don't hesitate! Like Calvin and Sandi, choose humility and take action to get free *now*!

Evil Slips in Through the Pages of a Magazine

In this brief testimony, Sheri from Houston shares how spiritual housecleaning freed her from freakish dreams and restless nights:

> For years I had been tormented by demonic dreams, and in these dreams I would battle demons and wake up hoarse from screaming, "In Jesus' name, you must go!" This was ongoing almost nightly.
>
> As we began our spiritual housecleaning, the Lord brought me to this magazine advertisement that I had cut out years earlier and had hanging on my desk cabinet at the foot of my bed. It was an encouraging ad, I thought. It pictured a man running with one leg and the other was made of a thin metal rod with a tennis shoe attached. It said, "Run your race and do not quit," and something about the heart of a champion.
>
> Trying to be sensitive to the voice of the Holy Spirit, as I approached the picture, the hair on my arms stood straight up and I got a sick feeling in my stomach. I removed the picture and turned it over to find a picture of a demon. It was the advertisement for *Spawn*, a movie subtitled *Spawn of Satan*. Needless to say, I prayed as I tore it to pieces. To this day I am no longer tormented by these dreams! Hallelujah!

What mistake did Sherri make? How did she discover the problem?

_____
_____
_____
_____
_____
_____
_____

How did Sheri deal with the problem?

_____

_____

_____

_____

_____

_____

_____

_____

Read and write out 1 Corinthians 6:12 and 10:23.

_____

_____

_____

_____

_____

_____

_____

How do these verses apply to spiritual housecleaning?

_____

_____

_____

_____

_____

_____

For years, we had a decorative box on our coffee table. One day, we discovered that the beautiful decoration on the cover consisted of small demonic images. We immediately discarded it. Do you think it would be a good idea for you to reexamine your possessions with a more careful eye?

_____

_____

_____

Only with the Lord's discernment and wisdom will we be able to effectively clean house. To do anything less is to operate out of the flesh (our lower Adamic nature), in a spirit of suspicion, superstition and paranoia—and that's not what God wants for our lives. He came to give us abundant Christian life (see John 10:10)! If you're having nightmares, experiencing demonic attacks or feeling anything oppressive in your home, *pray* and ask the Lord to reveal the root of the oppression to you. He is *faithful* and He has the answers you need to get free from fear and oppression.

In the Least Likely Places

Rose, another reader of *Spiritual House Cleaning*, asked the Lord to reveal the root of the oppression that lingered in her home. She had cleaned house but still found it hard to pray, so she asked the Lord to uncover any spiritually dark and offensive thing still hidden in her home. She wrote to us and described her experience:

> I purchased and read your book *Spiritual House Cleaning* because I found it very difficult to pray in my newly purchased townhome. I'd previously had several friends come to my home and pray over it, and we conducted spiritual housecleaning but there was still a hindrance.
>
> After reading your book, I asked the Holy Spirit to uncover any ungodly thing that remained. A few days later, I asked some workers who were in my attic to tell me if any boxes or items were in the attic that weren't part of my small cluster of stored boxes. The workmen found a box that they brought down to me. Inside the unfamiliar box was an Aztec god chess set and books on the paranormal. I was shocked! They must have been left by the previous owners.
>
> Finding that junk was an answer to my prayers. I broke all contracts with these items and my home, and asked the Lord's blessing. I now hold an AGLOW Lighthouse Intercessory prayer meeting in my home. Thanks so much for making the book available. May God continue to bless you abundantly.

Does this mean that we are to turn our houses upside down in search of potentially dangerous hidden objects? Are we bound to suffer needlessly because of devilish trinkets that other people left behind? Obviously, the answer is no. Isaiah 54:17 says, "No weapon forged against you will prevail" (*NIV*). As believers, we have the power to overcome the plots and schemes of the evil one—and to discern them. But we should ask the Lord to reveal them to us. When we don't ask, we don't receive. And there are times the devil will take advantage of our ignorance if we're not observant (see 2 Corinthians 2:11).

What did Rose do when she realized that there was still a spiritual hindrance in her home?

_____

_____

_____

_____

_____

_____

_____

What did the Holy Spirit do in response to her prayers?

_____

_____

_____

_____

_____

_____

_____

But my things are innocent, you might think. *Why would God want me to get rid of things that make me happy or that have sentimental value?* But seemingly innocent, "fun" interests, activities and objects, as we'll see in the next testimony, can sometimes lead us into temptation and torment.

What Are You Watching?

In the following testimony, a man named Chuck told us how he was able
to trace his angry attitude back to violent movie videos:

> I remember when your book came out. It was an instant best-
> seller. I had received my copy but had not read it. After all, I
> didn't have anything in my house or life that needed cleaning
> up—or so I thought. My Lord had already begun a wonderful
> work in my life and had brought me a long way from where I
> had been. But I thought, *Could there be anything else that need-
> ed attention?*
>
> It was fall of 2003. My wife had gone on a trip to see her
> mother, and I had the weekend alone. The Lord had been deal-
> ing with me about total commitment, so it was good to have
> the opportunity to pray and seek His will in my life.
>
> I remember on Friday evening as I was praying that I had
> a strong impression to read *Spiritual House Cleaning*. I said,
> "Well, all right, Lord, if that is what You want me to do." As I
> read, I learned many things I didn't know that have helped me
> understand circumstances that have come my way as prayer
> assignments. But that wasn't the reason I was supposed to
> read this book. The Lord had something very special for me
> that evening. On page 60 there was a simple phrase that
> changed my life for eternity.
>
> Eddie and Alice listed "Sources of Defilement." As I read
> the list, I remember reading and feeling a little smug and self-
> righteous. None of those things were in my life. I turned the
> page and continued reading each line and almost saying out
> loud, "That's not me."
>
> Until I read the line "Movies with occult messages and/or
> extreme violence." I think my heart skipped a beat and I read it
> again—"extreme violence." Then I heard myself say out loud,
> "But I love violent movies, the more violent the better."
>
> That's when God began speaking to me. "Do you love these
> things more than Me?"

"No! You know that I love You more than any movie, Lord."

That evening I made a commitment to my Lord that He is first in my life and that if that was displeasing to Him, I would not watch violent movies. But wouldn't you know it; the enemy saw this as an opportunity to tempt me. I never knew there were so many violent movies. They would pop up every time I turned the TV on.

You may be wondering why Jesus Christ didn't want me watching these kinds of movies, and at first I didn't understand either. Sometimes we just have to trust the leading of the Holy Spirit in our lives. I have long ago learned that the Lord has a plan and purpose for my life, and when I don't understand, I simply trust Him to lead.

What my Lord has worked in my life is this: He has made me a tenderhearted and compassionate man. I now understand that those violent movies were destroying what God wanted to do in me. There was a time when I had the emotions of a stone and the compassion of a wild hog. Now God has changed all that and He has given me a compassion that makes me cry out for this lost and dying world. I can honestly say that my life now is far better because of what Jesus has done. Thank You, Lord! And thank you, Eddie and Alice, for writing *Spiritual House Cleaning*.

What changes took place in Chuck's life as a result of him searching his heart—and his home—for spiritual pollution?

_____

_____

_____

_____

_____

_____

_____

_____

_____

Are there any negative behavior patterns, attitudes or addictions that you, or anyone in your household, can't seem to control or change? Describe them here.

_____
_____
_____
_____
_____
_____
_____

Have you asked the Lord if there might be anything in your home or any habits in your life that promote such behavior? What steps will you take to see change?

_____
_____
_____
_____
_____
_____
_____
_____

If not, take a few minutes now to ask the Holy Spirit. What do you sense Him putting on your heart?

_____
_____
_____
_____
_____
_____
_____

Or perhaps you have a story of personal victory in this area. If so, write out a prayer of thanksgiving for what God has done in your life.

_____

_____

_____

_____

_____

_____

Read Deuteronomy 7:25-26. What do these verses communicate about coveting what the world esteems?

_____

_____

_____

_____

_____

Again, this is not about superstition, paranoia or legalism. It's about being obedient and honoring God with all of our heart, soul, mind and strength (see Deuteronomy 6:5; Mark 12:30)—*and* it's about our possessions. It's our having lives and homes that leave no room for the devil to get a foothold and establishing environments of light, peace and joy in our areas of influence.

As we'll learn in the chapters to come, our children experience the effects of these things more tangibly than we adults do. Cleaning your home of forbidden objects opens the door of God's blessing to you and your family. But above all, it brings God glory!

Note

1. A pagoda is a tiered tower with multiple eaves common in many parts of Asia. Most pagodas were built for a religious function, most commonly Buddhist, and were often located in or near temples. The modern pagoda is an evolution of the Indian *stupa*, a tomb-like structure where sacred relics could be kept safe and venerated. Pagodas attract lightning strikes because of their height, which may have played a role in their perception as spiritually charged places. Many pagodas have a decorated finial at the top. The finial is designed to have symbolic meaning within Buddhism; for example, it may include designs representing a lotus. The finial also functions as a lightning rod and thus helps to both attract lightning and protect the pagoda from lightning damage. See "Pagoda," *Wikipedia*, March 23, 2007. http://en.wikipedia.org/wiki/Pagoda (accessed March 2007).

CHAPTER 3

Biblical Stories of Spiritual Housecleaning

Through the ages, God has had to clean house with His people. Secret sins, the flood, plagues, idolatry, ungodly covenants, forbidden marriages and blatant defiance have led God to scour the spiritual house of His people. So severe were their sins at times that the Lord took serious measures to bring His people back to a place of purity: measures that included destruction of ungodly objects, uncovering wicked lifestyles, the loss of a ministry or—unusual as it may seem—death to the rebellious.

The following accounts culled from both the Old and New Testaments reflect God's heart for holiness and His desire to have a people completely set apart for Himself. Take time to read carefully through each passage. Reflect on the events that occurred, on what the problem was, on how God and the people addressed the problem, and on what the end results were. After reading each biblical account, pause to think about your own life. How can you apply what you learn from these examples to keep your home and heart spiritually clean?

Defiled: Burning Bridges from the Devil

"When this became known to the Jews and Greeks living in Ephesus, they were all seized with fear, and the name of the Lord Jesus was held in high honor. Many of those who believed now came and openly confessed their evil deeds. A number who had practiced sorcery brought their scrolls together and burned them publicly. When they calculated the value of the scrolls, the total came to fifty thousand drachmas. In this way the word of the Lord spread widely and grew in power" (Acts 19:17-20, *NIV*).

What did the believers in Ephesus, those who had previously practiced magic, feel compelled to do?

_____

_____

_____

_____

_____

What practices were the Ephesian Christians involved in? What did the apostle Paul tell them to do?

_____

_____

_____

_____

_____

_____

What can we conclude about their actions (see v. 20)?

_____

_____

_____

_____

_____

What from this biblical story can you apply to your own life? What actions will you take?

_____

_____

_____

_____

_____

Consider the example of the Ephesian church. The believers burned their books of sorcery and witchcraft and experienced a release of the power of God among them. It appears that as a result of their righ-teous book burning, the Holy Spirit empowered them to impact their community in a profoundly more significant way than they had before: "The Word of God grew mightily and prevailed!" (Acts 19:20, *KJ21*).

A modern-day example of what happened in Ephesus took place in a rural part of Illinois when a former Wicca high priestess stumbled upon the book *Spiritual House Cleaning*. She tells the following story:

I was walking around the Christian bookstore praying earnestly for the Holy Spirit to lead me to a book that would help and encourage me. What an answer to prayer when I spotted a thin blue book entitled *Spiritual House Cleaning: Protect Your Home and Family from Spiritual Pollution*. This powerful little book confirmed what the Holy Spirit had taught and brought me through over the previous year.

Fourteen years before, I had become a rebellious pastor's daughter and turned my back on God for 10 long years. One day while walking around a secular bookstore I discovered the New Age section. I picked up a book on magic just for fun and started following the directions so easily laid out for me by the author. To my amazement, it worked! I tried another spell, then another and soon I was hooked!

Soon after, I bought my first set of tarot cards and read fortunes for many people from that day forward. I hungered for more and more. I started searching the Internet and found a group of Wiccans (witches) who were 30 miles away and had a wonderful metaphysical store where I could purchase my magical supplies.

I joined them and soon earned the title of High Priestess and was teaching others. But something was missing. I remember one day just sitting outside saying to myself, *Is this it? Is this all there is to Wicca? Where are those so-called ancient mysteries?* All I had been taught was garbage. Good old Satan, truly the master deceiver, has stolen 10 years of my life and filled them with an empty, false religion, but I kept plugging away hoping it would get better. Instead I became emptier and angrier at life.

Then, one January, I was flipping through the stations on the television and stopped on a Christian broadcast. I cannot tell you who the preacher was or what the message was—I just knew that I needed Jesus! I turned off the TV and knelt beside my couch and cried out to God and He came and forgave me and set me free from the occult!

I knew that I needed to get rid of all of my occult things. A few days later, I went to the burn barrel on our farm and started burning books, wands, staffs, robes, herbs and other paraphernalia. I recalled Acts 19:18-20: "Many of those who believed now came and openly confessed their evil deeds. A number who had practiced sorcery brought their scrolls together and burned them publicly. When they calculated the value of the scrolls, the total came to fifty thousand drachmas. In this way the word of the Lord spread widely and grew in power."

Wow! That is my testimony. I do not know the value of what I burnt that day, but it all added to more than I care to recall.

I still had a few things that I was not quite willing to part with, namely my tarot cards. How I loved them and how I depended on them for all my answers! God dealt with me on this matter. I told Him, "Lord, I love You and thank You for setting me free, but I love my cards, I need them. I've read the Bible all the way through many times, Lord, but it never really did much for me. So, Lord, until you make the Bible come alive to me, like these cards, I cannot part with them."

Do you know that the God of the universe loved me so much that He actually heard and answered my ignorant prayer ? I read my Bible every day. To my surprise the Word of God was becoming more and more alive to me! In fact, the Bible gave me answers in detail unlike anything the cards ever gave me. Then about a month went by and I said, "Lord! Do You realize that I have not picked up my cards in about a month? I have only needed Your Word!" And the Lord said, "Yes, now burn them."

I obediently bundled up and headed out on that blizzard morning to my burn barrel. The cards took a long time to burn. I believe God made the winds flip each card one at a time and hit the side of the barrel and then slowly melt. The meaning of each card went through my mind as I watched it melt and watched the grotesque yellowy-black smoke rise into the dreary sky. I stood there shivering, waiting for the last card to melt and disappear. Then I walked away.

When I reached the other side of my farmhouse, I noticed that the snow had stopped and the sun had come out. I looked over the field of freshly fallen new snow. How beautiful it was as it sparkled like a million small diamonds. Then I heard my Savior whisper, "Michelle, this is your heart now. I have washed it as white as this snow. You are free!"

Spiritual housecleaning is the key to true freedom!

Defiled: Breaking Ungodly Covenants

Read 2 Samuel 21:1-14. David—and the whole nation of Israel—had a serious problem. Having suffered through three years of famine, the king was desperate for the reason why. When he cried out to God for the answer, the Lord revealed the reason His people were in such a dire situation: Sins of the past—sins that David and the current generation were likely unaware of—had defiled the land, bringing the wrath of God upon it. Although it may seem strange to us, when David learned this, he took immediate action to rectify the wrongs Israel had committed and to make right a broken promise.

What was the problem?

_____

_____

_____

_____

_____

_____

How did David respond to this national crisis? (In other words, did he seek men's counsel or God's counsel?) What was his first course of action?

_____

_____

_____

_____

_____

_____

What did David discover that had produced the problem?

_____

_____

_____

_____

_____

_____

Looking at the following passages, identify what defiled the land:

Exodus 34:12-17: _____

Leviticus 18:22-25: _____

Deuteronomy 12:2-3: _____

1 Kings 14:21-24: _____

Psalm 79:1-3: _____

Psalm 74:8-10: _____

Psalm 106:34-39: _____

Isaiah 24:5: _____

Jeremiah 3:1-3,9: _____

Actually, there were *two* issues. What was Israel's first mistake, and why was it an offense to God (see 2 Samuel 21:2 and Joshua 9)?

_____

_____

_____

_____

_____

_____

_____

What did Saul do to compound the sin that Israel initially committed? (There's no actual passage describing the story other than David's account in 2 Samuel.)

_____

_____

_____

_____

_____

What corrective steps did David take to clean up the situation?

_____

_____

_____

_____

_____

What happened as a result of David's acts of repentance (see v. 14)?

_____

_____

_____

_____

_____

Defiled: Undoing Blood Covenants

Read 2 Kings 24:4, Psalms 94:21 and 106:38, Proverbs 6:17 and Matthew 27:3-5. These kinds of accounts aren't limited to what we read in Scripture. Current, real-life examples of those who've cleaned house God's way come to us all the time. Here, a young man writes to tell us how he used the principles he learned from *Spiritual House Cleaning* to break free from an ungodly covenant and from the chains of Satanism and suicide:

I first heard about *Spiritual House Cleaning: Protect Your Home and Family from Spiritual Pollution* in May 2005 and I knew that I needed to do it.

I started praying and the Lord started showing me things. At this time I was very bound by Satan, having been a Satanist for many years. I was on 16 different psychiatric meds at the time and constantly wanted to kill myself. I felt that there was no hope and that no one wanted me. The Lord showed me that cleaning house was the next step in getting free.

As I started the process of spiritual housecleaning, the first thing I came across was blood from a blood covenant that I had made with my brother before he died. I could not let go of him. After destroying this, however, I was no longer plagued with evil thoughts of my brother and could finally say goodbye.

There were many things I got rid of that day, and as I destroyed each thing my heart got lighter and the depression started leaving.

Upon completing my spiritual housecleaning, I could tell that something had happened in my heart. I was set free from the things of my past. Within one month the doctors took me off of 10 of those medicines. And I went from being on a psych ward at least twice a month to not going for months at a time. When I look back, I see that getting rid of the things that did not glorify God was the turning point in my life.

In your personal life, have you made any covenants with others that dishonor God? If so, what are they? Or have you broken promises to God? Have you made any unfulfilled pledges to God or others (e.g., unpaid traffic tickets, personal loans, student loans, rent, or credit card debt)?

_____

_____

_____

_____

_____

_____

If you've broken vows you've made to God or others and you haven't re-pented for them, take a moment now to stop and ask God for forgiveness. Ask the Lord to show you what corrective actions you need to take to restore your relationship with Him and with others (see Ecclesiastes 5:5). Are there any objects in your possession that represent those covenants or broken promises? What is the Holy Spirit telling you to do with them?

_____
_____
_____
_____
_____

In faith and obedience, take the steps necessary to rid those things from your life. You might have to give them back to a previous owner, throw them away or destroy them completely. Once you've done that, take time to reflect on any changes that have occurred in your home, church and/or life as a result of your obedience. Write down the changes that you have observed, and make sure to thank God for those positive results!

_____
_____
_____
_____
_____
_____

Defiled: Carrying Out the Uncleanness

Read 2 Chronicles 29. Hezekiah was a king who did right in the sight of God. He began his reign by opening the doors of the house of the Lord and repairing them. He wanted the condition of God's house to reflect a spirit of reverence and honor toward Him. Before inviting any-one in to worship there, he gathered the priests and commissioned them to take on one very intense housecleaning project. He acknowl-edged the sins of their fathers and repented for them. He knew that a key to Israel's peace and prosperity lay in the cleanliness of their hearts as well as in that of their house of worship.

What does it mean to "consecrate" someone or something?

_____

_____

_____

_____

_____

_____

Why did Hezekiah tell the Levites to consecrate both themselves and the Temple?

_____

_____

_____

_____

_____

_____

What did Hezekiah tell the priests to remove from the holy place (see v. 5)?

_____

_____

_____

_____

_____

_____

What evil did the "fathers" do to require such a cleansing of the Temple (see v. 6.)?

_____

_____

_____

_____

_____

According to verses 9 and 10, what resulted from the sins of the fathers?

_____

_____

_____

_____

_____

What did the priests do in response to Hezekiah's desire to repent on behalf of Israel (see vv. 15-17)?

_____

_____

_____

_____

How long did this process take (see v. 17)? (Not quite a speedy cleaning, was it?) Explain here.

_____

_____

_____

_____

What was required when the priests "purged the altar" (see v. 24)?

_____

_____

_____

_____

What blood sacrifice was required as a basis for purifying people's homes?

_____

_____

_____

_____

How did they complete the cleansing process?

_____

_____

_____

_____

_____

From this passage, what can we learn about the significance of *worship* in the spiritual housecleaning process?

_____

_____

_____

_____

_____

What was reestablished as a result of Hezekiah's housecleaning?

_____

_____

_____

_____

_____

How did the people respond (see v. 28)?

_____

_____

_____

_____

_____

What has the Lord shown you through this story?

_____

_____

_____

_____

_____

Defiled: Exposing Forbidden Treasure

Read Joshua 7. At Jericho, still savoring the taste of their greatest victory in the Promised Land and expecting nothing less for their future, the Israelites must have felt fearless. Joshua's scouts had told him that only two or three thousand men would be necessary to destroy Ai and its people, so he did not anticipate that the army of Ai would swoop down on his men and overwhelm them completely. After all, the town of Ai means "a heap of ruin," so the Israelites certainly weren't intimidated. What led to this slaughter after such sweet success?

The answer lay back home, hidden in the darkness of *one man's* tent: He had stolen treasure from Jericho that God had strictly prohibited (see Joshua 6:17-19) and thus brought condemnation on the whole community. The penalty for his rebellion led to the death of 36 Israelites and the humiliation of the entire nation.

Shocked and broken, Joshua and the elders cried out to the Lord, asking Him what went wrong and why He allowed them to be so heavily defeated. One more defeat like this and all Israel could be easily wiped out by the Canaanites. In this passage, we see the seriousness of God's commands and the severity of the punishment that came upon the disobedient.

What was the problem, and why couldn't Israel defeat the men of Ai (see Joshua 11:12)?

_____

_____

_____

_____

_____

Note how *one person's sin* can affect everyone else in his or her home, church or business. We also must realize that disobeying the Lord and His commands leads to the loss of His blessing and protection. What did God tell Joshua to do in order to purge Israel of the sin in the camp?

_____

_____

_____

_____

What was the result? Continue to read the first few verses of Joshua 8 to see how God honored the Israelites' obedience.

_____

_____

_____

_____

_____

Thankfully, today, you and I can *expose our secret sins* and forbidden treasures and *be cleansed by* the blood of Jesus. His mercy and His grace swallow up our iniquity so that the ground doesn't have to. There are consequences, however, for worshiping idols and hanging on to ungodly possessions.

Are there any idols in your life or home? They could be physical (e.g., a statue of Mary or Buddha or an object considered sacred by a cult or false religion) or intangible (e.g., living out forbidden fantasies in your mind, worshiping wealth or idolizing another person). Write down any such things here.

_____

_____

_____

_____

_____

When we ask the Lord to show us the causes behind oppression in our lives, homes, churches and businesses, He is faithful to reveal them. Now would be a good time to pray and ask the Lord what steps to take to rid yourself of these things. What do you sense the Holy Spirit telling you to do?

_____

_____

_____

_____

_____

10 Key Lessons from Joshua 7

1. God's Promises to Us Are Awesome!
Looking back at the story of Achan's sin and Israel's repentance, we can learn several significant lessons and apply them to our own lives. One is the *faithfulness* of God—He keeps His promises and His promises are awesome.

Read 2 Peter 1:3-4. What does it say about God's promises toward us?

_____

_____

_____

_____

2. God's Promises Are Often Contingent upon Our Obedience
Do you know that we have to take responsibility for some of the promises God gives us? We have a part to play in receiving certain things that He wants to give us. As we wrote in *Spiritual House Cleaning*, "His promises are activated by our faith. However, many of God's promises are conditional. They are contingent upon our obedience. We call them God's If/Then promises."[1]

Read Joshua 1:1-15, Romans 10:9 and 1 John 1:9. What are the "if/thens" that you see in these passages?

_____

_____

_____

_____

_____

Achan disobeyed God's commands by taking for himself things that God had designated for destruction. Because he (including all Israel) didn't fulfill his part of the promise, God briefly removed His hand of protection from over them and devastation came. We see, then, that it is imperative that we are careful to do all that God commands, knowing that disobedience and the worship of anything other than God bring a curse.

3. Physical Things Sometimes Carry Spiritual Significance
Take a look at the following passages: Exodus 12:7-13, Numbers 21:5-9, Matthew 26:28, Luke 3:21-22, Acts 19:11-12 and James 5:14.

What connections do you see between physical objects and spiritual principles in these Scriptures?

_____

_____

_____

_____

_____

Turn back to Numbers 21. Why did Moses originally make the bronze serpent? What was its purpose?

_____

_____

_____

_____

_____

Now go to 2 Kings 18:4. How was the intended use of the bronze serpent corrupted?

_____

_____

_____

_____

_____

Placing faith in *anything* or *anyone* other than God and His Word is idolatry. And some things, whether we worship them or not, carry spiritual significance of a demonic nature. So while we're not in the business of superstition or paranoia, we are concerned with living clean before God—and that means making sure that the things we possess and hold dear have nothing demonic attached to them.

4. There Are Certain Things That We Are Forbidden to Possess
What do 2 Corinthians 5:27 and Ephesians 5:8-11 say about our new life in Christ?

_____

_____

_____

_____

_____

In the Old Testament, God clearly communicated to the Israelites that they were to have no other gods and no physical images that they worshiped (see Exodus 20:3; Deuteronomy 4:15-19,23-24). This is still true for us today! Objects that represent other gods or that draw power from any source other than God (in other words, from demons) have absolutely no place in a believer's life. "Such objects are strictly forbidden, because they open the door to supernatural deception, turn people away from God and hinder people's spiritual and physical health."[2]

5. The Use of an Item Can Establish Its Spiritual Significance
What does Paul have to say about idols in 1 Corinthians 8:3-13 and 10:19-20?

_____

_____

_____

_____

_____

Human beings make some objects for the express purpose of being worshiped and/or used to channel demons, while other things become objects of idolatry because of the value and power a particular owner or culture ascribes to them. In either case, such objects can bring chaos into our lives because of their association with the demonic world—and the Lord does not want His people fellowshipping with the demons (see 1 Corinthians 10:20).

6. Illicit Possessions Can Separate Us from God's Purposes, Protection and Power

God's protection and His power are released through us as part of His purposes for us. "When we willfully—or ignorantly for that matter—step away from God's purposes for our lives, we step out from under His protective care."[3]

How do you see this principle at work in Samson's life, as described in Judges 16?

_____

_____

_____

_____

_____

_____

7. One Person's Crime Can Create Corporate Guilt and Result in Corporate Consequences

Go back to Joshua 7 and note down all the times God uses a corporate reference (e.g., "Israel," "them" or "they") rather than an individual one (e.g., "Achan").

_____

_____

_____

_____

_____

_____

_____

While individual responsibility for corporate cursing (or blessing) might be foreign to Westerners, it's a principle clearly laid out in Scripture. We are part of Christ's Body and individually members of it (see 1 Corinthians 12:26; Ephesians 3:6; 4:25; 5:30; Colossians 3:15). What we do, say and *possess* affects our families, churches, friends and colleagues. Shouldn't we bring blessings rather than curses to those we're corporately bound to?

8. When We Seek God, He Will Reveal the Defiled Things
What does John 16:13 say the Holy Spirit will do for us?

_____

_____

_____

_____

_____

Look up 1 Corinthians 2:16 and Ephesians 1:17. What do these verses tell us about God's desire to illuminate the darkness for us?

_____

_____

_____

_____

_____

God doesn't want us living in deception and ignorance but promises to reveal unknown things to us if we ask Him (see Jeremiah 33:3). And because of Christ's sacrifice on the cross, we do not have to pay a penalty like Achan and his family did. However, to live truly victorious, powerful lives and to safeguard ourselves, our families and our churches from demonic oppression, we must do away with ungodly objects.

9. We Should Ruthlessly Rid Ourselves of Wicked Things
We musn't give mere lip service to God—all that we do and all that we have reflects what we're truly about. If we're about Christ and His kingdom, our lives and possessions ought to reflect His holiness, love, peace and joy. When the Lord reveals something to us that doesn't line up with this, we must act swiftly and thoroughly to remove it, be it from our hearts or homes or both. The devil is unrelenting in his hatred toward us; we, therefore, must be unrelenting in ridding our lives of anything that

glorifies him. And remember, the flipside is also true: God's unrelenting love for you ought to compel you to do all to honor Him.

10. Obedience Restores Our Fellowship with God and Reinstates His Purposes

Read Joshua 8. What happened to Joshua and the children of Israel after they repented and took the necessary steps to cleanse their camp of the offensive objects (and of the offenders)?

_____

_____

_____

_____

_____

Do you want the full measure of God's presence, peace, power, provision and protection in your life? Then follow Joshua's example. Although it might be painful for a moment, it will be well worth it when you are right with God and able to receive the victory and the blessings He wants to lead you into.

Purify and Prevail

Read Genesis 35:1-7. What did God tell Jacob and his family to do before they set out on their journey to Bethel?

_____

_____

_____

_____

_____

What did Jacob do to honor God?

_____

_____

_____

_____

Note how they purified themselves, got rid of their idols and became a terror to their enemies without even lifting a finger to them!

Do you have any idols that God is calling you to get rid of? What might be the result if you removed such things from your life?

_____

_____

_____

_____

_____

_____

In the following chapters you'll read stories of those who put these principles to work, purified themselves and "put away the foreign gods" that held them in bondage. Having read *Spiritual House Cleaning*, they had the tools necessary to rid their lives, homes, churches and work places of spiritual darkness and to close trapdoors that the enemy was using to gain access to them. Their stories testify, just as these biblical stories do, to the power and greatness of God and to the authority we, as believers, have in Him to live abundantly free, victorious lives.

Notes
1. Eddie and Alice Smith, *Spiritual House Cleaning* (Ventura, CA: Regal Books, 2003), p. 19.
2. Ibid., p. 25.
3. Ibid., p. 28.

CHAPTER 4

Children and Spiritual Housecleaning

Pastor Rene De La Cruz, from California, shared with us the following experience about an anxious father who pleaded for help for his child:

On a cold fall evening in 2002, at about 8 P.M., I was all alone studying in my office. My private line rang, and as I picked up the phone a feeling of dread came over me. In broken English, a man with a Hispanic accent said, "Hello? Is this the children's pastor? My baby needs help! Please help my baby!" I could hear a baby screaming in the background.

The man began to tell me that he and his wife had just moved into the area. The couple, their three children, a grandmother and one brother had just moved from Guatemala. He began to tell me that just a few days ago, his one-year-old son began screaming for no apparent reason. He said that the baby had not been able to eat or sleep for about eight days, but the moment they took their child out of the apartment, the baby would settle down, eat and then fall asleep. The couple took the child to a physician and he ran multiple tests. All the tests came back negative—the baby was given a clean bill of health and released.

As the parents walked out of the hospital, a nurse followed them out and whispered to the mother, "Your baby is being harassed by a demon. You must call a pastor." Apparently this man picked up the phone and dialed our church. The man begged for me to come and to pray for his child. I agreed, but first I told him to hold his child in his arms, because I was going to pray for his son over the phone. I prayed this prayer over the child, "In Jesus' name, I command this harassing spirit to leave this child alone. I command you to set this child free!" I took down his address and I called Tony, a fellow intercessor.

We pulled up to an old apartment complex and found the unit number. I knocked on the door and the distraught father answered and invited us in. There on the floor was their baby boy sleeping and breathing heavily, surrounded by their entire family. The father told me that their child fell asleep about five minutes after I prayed for him over the phone.

I felt a spirit of death over the apartment and I did a brief background check on the apartment complex. The man's brother told me that the back room was always cold and that he felt scared every time he was in that particular room, so scared that he slept on the couch in the living room. As he was talking, I stopped and asked, "Were there any crimes committed here?" The brother spoke out and said, "Some man was killed right here, before we moved in."

Then the grandmother began to tell of stories of lights flickering and strange noises coming from the empty bedrooms. The two children shared stories of strange shadows that would move around the room.

I began to share how Satan looks for opportunities to harass people and how territorial spirits sometimes manifest themselves in an area where a crime has been committed. But the most important thing that I did was to share the gospel of Jesus Christ. After I shared a bit on spiritual warfare, I told them that they were powerless unless they received Jesus into their hearts. Before I knew it, the mom, dad, children, grandma and older brother all prayed to receive Jesus Christ. After that we went to every room of the apartment and cast out every foul spirit in the name of Jesus.

The following Sunday the entire family came to church, and to my knowledge the baby and family have not encountered any more strange occurrences in their home.

Isn't it exciting that what the devil intended for evil—to scare and intimidate this family and harass their innocent baby—God turned around and used for *good*? The enemy's plan was absolutely thwarted when this family not only rid their home of a demonic presence but also (and best of all) gave their lives to Christ and filled their home with *the presence of the Holy Spirit*!

In Luke 9:37-43, what did Jesus do to deliver the boy from the spirit that was tormenting him?

_____

_____

_____

_____

_____

_____

_____

_____

And what does Jesus say in John 14:12 about those who have faith in Him?

_____

_____

_____

_____

_____

_____

_____

_____

How did this pastor use his authority in Christ to send demons packing?

_____

_____

_____

_____

_____

_____

_____

What does Acts 19:13-16 indicate about those who try to cast out demons but don't know Christ?

_____

_____

_____

_____

_____

_____

_____

While all of us who are in Christ have this authority, why is it always wise to bring others with you and/or to have someone who has experience with demonic deliverance help you?

_____

_____

_____

_____

_____

_____

_____

What is the spiritual history of your home? What do you know about the previous owners or tenants? What do you know about the property on which your house or apartment sits? (Could it sit on a historical battlefield or ancient burial ground? This may require a trip to the local library.)

_____

_____

_____

_____

_____

_____

_____

Have your children demonstrated any patterns of behavior similar to those of this baby (e.g., uncontrollable crying, inability to sleep, fear of the dark or of being in a particular room, or a sense of something scary in the house)?

_____

_____

_____

_____

_____

_____

_____

There Is a Battle for Our Children

A spiritual battle is being waged for the souls of our children. Since the beginning of time, this has been the case, but never has the enemy worked so deviously and on so many fronts to destroy a young generation. We really have to consider this battle from two standpoints: the media and our homes.

First, America's homes are under attack and are being invaded by insidious spiritual forces through various media. Evil spirits seek entrance into the privacy of our homes through music, computer images, video games and movies, books, magazines and television shows—all negatively affecting our children. Rappers indoctrinate our children to exploit women as sex objects and to have no respect for family, government, God or themselves. Friends tempt them to engage in sexual promiscuity at earlier and earlier ages and entice them with alcohol, nicotine and drugs. Liberal public schools disregard the need for God (we thank the Lord for the godly teachers who continue to stay in these schools as a direct act of obedience to Him). At every turn, godly parents have to fight vigilantly to successfully contend with the godless world around their children.

Even in the godliest home, all it takes is for a child to go to an overnight slumber party with a friend whose father has a stash of porn or whose family subscribes to a cable movie channel and his or her life can be immediately altered forever.

Second, we have spiritually clueless parents who buy Abercrombie & Fitch thong underwear with the word "sexy" embroidered in sequins for their preteen daughters. Parents who buy such things are essentially acting as their daughters' pimps, throwing them to the corporate wolves who will force on them the most lurid, shocking, edgy products imaginable. To some parents, this abdication of parental responsibility is chic. After all, they don't want to appear uptight, overbearing, puritanical or judgmental. They'd rather be their children's friends than their moral compass and protector. Parents must wake up and see that America's ugly, shallow, gutter culture is destroying the souls of our children.

Thank God for pastors, churches, specialized ministries and key intercessors who are aware of the spiritual battle we face and who are stepping into the battle as spiritual strategists to provide divine solutions for our children. As parents, we must do the same. Satan takes advantage of every opportunity to steal, kill and destroy. We cannot remain naïve to the fact that this is exactly what the devil wants to do to our children and their generation. It's our responsibility to rise up and fight for them—to do everything in our power to see them become powerful men and women who advance the Kingdom of light and not cultural converts who blindly stumble into the kingdom of darkness.

This Intense Battle Is Specifically Directed at Their Minds

Tereasa Knicely shares the following story:

> One day many years ago, my daughter Sarah was given a Japanese toy by our neighbor who had just come back from visiting her Japanese homeland. It was a strange toy, and I felt that it had some "odd" feelings attached to it.
>
> The next morning, Sarah told me about a strange dream she had, and it involved the Japanese toy. It was a very evil and eerie dream. I told her that a lot of times Asian toys are designed in the images of the idols they worship, such as Buddha, Amitabha, Maitreya, Dharma, Sangha, Krishna, Shiva, Kali, Brahman, Vishnu, Shakti, Ganesh, and others. Most often, evil spirits stay attached to the idols to keep the seekers deceived. My daughter

Sarah understood and without hesitation threw the toy in the trash. No more bad dreams.

Another time, Sarah was playing a Zelda video game. *The Legend of Zelda: The Twilight Princess* is part of a popular series of Nintendo video games that involves demons, wizards, ghosts, temples and curses. I carefully watched her play it a few times and then mentioned to Sarah that some of the signs in the game were from the occult and she had better be careful.

She said, "Don't worry, Mom. I can handle it." Over the next six to eight months, however, her anger turned into fits of temper tantrums—at times she ripped holes in our screens and once slammed a door into a wall so hard that the knob went right through it. Right away the Lord prompted me that the Zelda video game opened the door, affecting her mind and provoking her to rage. I, too, was to blame for allowing my family to have such a game when I felt convicted from the beginning of its occult signs.

I explained all this to Sarah and insisted that she throw it away. I did not want to give it to anyone else, even though being a collector's edition it had cost me more than $300. Thereafter, I noticed that her mind was clearer and her attitude changed. Praise God!

Tools the Enemy Uses to Entrap and Defile Our Children

As Tereasa points out, toys and video games are at the top of the list of things that can entrap and defile our children. *Why? What could be wrong with toys and video games? They're just child's play, right?* Some are—some aren't!

British author J. K. Rowling has indoctrinated a whole generation of children with the devices of devils through her series of Harry Potter books. Unlike some fairy tales where there's a wicked witch who dies because of her malevolence, Rowling's witch is the *central figure of the story*! Harry Potter himself not only lives, but he also thrives! *He's the one* the child reader emulates and bonds with. And Rowling's first six books have collectively sold more than 350 million copies and have been translated into 47 languages.

Having worked in the area of helping people find deliverance from demonic spirits for more than 35 years, we wouldn't expect there to be much demonic manifestation as a result of this. No. Demons just don't operate that way. They typically linger for 10 to 20 years and then—when the child reaches his or her teen years or adulthood and begins to establish a family and find a meaningful career—the demons he or she contracted as a child begin to surface and destroy his or her life, relationships and influence.

When the Battle Begins

The battle for our children begins *before conception* because demonic spirits often move from one generation to the next through what we call *generational iniquity*. Not only do the sins of the parents affect generations to come (see Exodus 20:5; 34:5-7; Deuteronomy 5:9; 7:10; Matthew 23:32-36; 1 Thessalonians 2:16; 1 Peter 1:18), but also demons that were attached to the parents often move to the children to maintain their grip (see Hosea 4:12-13).

Quite often the battle begins with a preschool child who is sexually molested. For example, when Joni was five years old, her uncle's wife left him because of his adulterous relationship with one of her friends. When she kicked him out of the house, he moved in with Joni's family for six months. During the night he would visit Joni's room. In her innocence, Joni didn't understand what her uncle was doing to her; and although what was done to her was painful and confusing, she was afraid to tell anyone. Later, when she learned that he had sexually abused her, she was embarrassed to tell anyone.

As Joni grew to adulthood, she found it hard to trust men. She tended to be defensive and frightened around them. However, during her second year in college she met, fell in love with and married a wonderful Christian man. One day during a casual conversation with her father, Joni learned that several of the men on her father's side of the family, like the uncle that molested her, were adulterers and one nephew was a practicing homosexual.

Then Joni realized why her children were struggling with their sexual identity. There was an iniquitous pattern that previous generations had established. It had opened the door to darkness in the family. After praying with her husband, Joni repented for the sins of her family (as Nehemiah repented for his father's in Nehemiah 9). Out loud, she broke the attachments to sexual sin and demonic activity associated with her family.

Signs That the Enemy Is Having Success with Children

With younger children, we typically see the following signs:

- Sleeplessness
- Recurring sickness
- Bad dreams
- Demonic appearances ("monsters in my room")[1]
- Lying
- Fear

Some signs of trouble usually exhibited by older children include:

- Rebellion and stubbornness
- Depression or withdrawal (anti-social)
- Verbal abuse
- Anger, temper or rage
- Manipulation or deceit
- Refusal to do household chores
- No interest in formerly productive activities, hobbies or sports
- Trouble at school (suspended, expelled, truant or shows a dramatic drop in grades)
- Trouble with the law
- Experimentation with drugs or alcohol
- Excessive piercings, cuttings, and so forth
- Tattoos of demonic images (gargoyles, dragons, skull and bones, snakes, evil expressions of faces)
- Loss of motivation
- Change in appearance or personal hygiene
- Sexual promiscuity

• Stealing (even from siblings and parents)
• Unwillingness to abide by basic family rules and expectations
• Association with the wrong friends or a bad peer group
• Signs of suicidal ideation

If Your Child Has Already Received Defiled Things

It's possible that your child already owns defiled things. Perhaps you were the one who bought them for him or her. If so, relax. We're all on a learning curve. God is revealing things to us by the day. The very fact that you are reading this book is evidence of your desire to know more about how to please God.

Let's face it: Life is about making midcourse corrections. It's on-the-job training. There are no schools to teach us parenting skills. Some people have suggested that if we must have a license to drive, to fish, to hunt and to get married, perhaps we should be required to get a license to have children.[2]

If you've provided unholy things for your children, and the Lord convicts you to confront them about those things, we feel that it's very important that you do this in love and humility. Explain to your child that you are learning what does and doesn't please the Lord and that the Lord is revealing things to you that the devil might use to harm them. Admit your ignorance in the matter. Ask them to forgive you. Ask your children to help you correct the problem in the home. If you learn to apologize to your children when you make a mistake, they are more likely to model the same behavior to you.

Ownership and House Rules

Before we begin, we want you to know that we hold to the principle of respecting ownership. There are two things to consider here: (1) your child (to some degree) owns his or her possessions; (2) you own (to some degree) your child, your home and what's in it. Hopefully you won't have to explain that to your child.

We taught our children that their rooms were in our house. We own the house—therefore, we own the rooms. They use the room, so to speak.

They can call a room theirs, but it is completely accessible to us at any time, for any purpose. They don't own the room—we do. With that in mind, we will have final say-so about what is in the room, what is on the walls, what type of music is played there—everything that is done in the room. Once they realize that everything is subject to review, accountability is established in their eyes. Always remember to be loving and kind. To be mean-spirited, cruel, rude or abusive to our children is sin and won't produce the desired results.

A note on respecting your child's privacy and property: Unless your child is grossly disrespectful, unmanageable, exhibits self-destructive behavior (e.g., acts suicidal, uses or hides drugs, and so forth) or may be a danger to others, we suggest that you not open their journals or diaries. Maintain the right to do so, however, if absolutely necessary.

Rules and limits are necessary for any successful society. It's important that both parents agree to the basic house rules. As long as the parents cannot agree, the child cannot be led. If the parents cannot agree on the rules, then what they are facing is a marriage problem, not a parenting problem. They should fix the marriage problem first.

Once that's done, the house rules should be clearly and appropriately presented to the child. The more compliant and responsive your child is, the fewer the rules you'll need. However, if your child is difficult or defiant, you'll need to provide a more defined structure.

The bottom line? *Responsiblity earns freedom. Irresponsiblity loses freedom.* Penitentiaries are filled with irresponsible people who've lost their freedom. Tell your children this, and if necessary offer examples so that they are clear about your guidelines. Most important, the house rules must:

- Be clearly communicated and understood
- Be monitored
- Be consistently enforced (say what you mean, and mean what you say)

In addition, *have consequences that are effective but in line with the offense.* For instance, one young couple came to us concerned because their five-year-old daughter tried to eat the soap at bath time. Deeply distressed over the matter, they explained how one of them had to keep an eye on her every moment during her baths.

Our suggestion? Let her eat the soap.

The mother objected, "No. She'll get an upset stomach."

"Certainly," we agreed. "But she'll never eat the soap again."

As you might guess, it worked. The consequences were effective. Obviously, this action isn't appropriate if it might endanger your child.

Another couple came to us because their three-year-old son was impervious to pain. Running in front of a car didn't scare him, and jumping out of a tree never fazed him. They explained, "He can fall down on the concrete, jump up and continue playing. Nothing hurts him! Even our spankings don't bring tears. We are at our wits' end."

We suggested that rather than spanking him, they take from him his most prized possession or activity as a consequence of his bad behavior. His favorite activity was art. The next time they had to correct him, they took away all of his crayons and coloring books for 24 hours. He burst into tears. It was punishment enough, and it worked!

Age-Appropriate Ways of Dealing with Unholy Possessions

How then do we approach our child concerning things that he or she possesses that are unfit for a young Christian? To a certain extent, this depends on one's opinion, but if our child were 2 years old, we'd deal with him differently from if he were 12 and differently if he were 16 or older.

Before talking to your child about getting rid of a possession, we suggest you discuss the reasons with him or her why all of us should be concerned about our possessions. Perhaps you could give your child an example of something the Lord asked you to discard. Talk *to* your child, not *down* to your child. Also exercise care that you don't create fear. Children have great imaginations and can be easily frightened. They can become superstitious as well. For that matter, so can parents!

Last year while we were teaching in Amsterdam, a lady asked me (Eddie) if she could get demons by picking up her son's dirty clothes. She explained that her older teen wasn't living for the Lord. She obviously thought he was demonized to some degree and was fearful of touching his possessions. The quick answer is, no, you can't. However, if she is filled with this much superstition and fear, she likely has a spiritual hole in her armor that could be taken advantage of by the enemy (compare Ephesians 4:27 and Romans 14:23 with 1 John 4:18). So avoid being superstitious and creating superstition. It's not mentally, spiritually or physically healthy.

Also, be careful not to teach your child to be judgmental of others. Explain that because the Lord told you to get rid of something that doesn't mean that you have the assignment to correct everyone else. You shouldn't attempt to enforce God's revelation to you on others. Your focus is to hear and obey God for yourself. Trust God to deal with others, but obviously, if someone asks for your advice, you are free to offer it.

The Four General Stages of Childhood

The following are the four general stages of child development:

1. Infancy (birth to age 2)
2. Early childhood (ages 3 to 8 years)
3. Later childhood (ages 9 to 12)
4. Adolescence (ages 13 to 18)

A child's learning capacity grows as he or she moves up through these four stages, and *the enemy's approach shifts through these developmental stages.*

Suggestions for Dealing with an Infant (Birth to Age 2)

Generally speaking, if your child is an infant, we suggest you secretly remove the object in question. You might offer a replacement toy. If it becomes necessary to explain, say something like, "Daddy and Mommy felt it was something that made Jesus unhappy, so we put it away. We'll look for something better to replace it." (Avoid terms such as "devil," "Satan," "demons" and "evil.")

Suggestions for Dealing with a Young Child (Ages 3 to 8)

Children from 3 to 8 years old are all different. Some understand more than others. Until the child is school age, avoid those "hot words" that can produce confusion, curiosity or fear. Instead of saying "devil" or "demons," use the phrase "bad things."

During these years, a child can be lovingly taught to respect what he or she has and how to discern whether something should or shouldn't be in his or her possession. When your child is between the ages of 6 and 8, you might even encourage your child to go through his or her own possessions with your help. Hold up each item and ask your child if he or she thinks the object honors or dishonors Christ. Try to make this a happy time; prepare special snacks during break time and read aloud a special prayer of dedication to God once the activity is over. Be creative. Deposit a good memory in your child's "memory bank."

Sherri Weeks from Houston, Texas, shares the following on how spiritual housecleaning affected her two young sons.

> After learning about spiritual housecleaning years ago, our family prayed and dedicated our home to the Lord. As we prayed, the Lord revealed specific objects or places in our home that we were to go to. The first place He led us was to our VHS collection of Disney/children's videos. We laid them all out on our couch and prayed over each one. As we came to the movie *Bedknobs and Broomsticks,* the Lord spoke to our eight-year-old son and said to get rid of that now! Our son told us that we should not have this movie—we all agreed, sensing the same thing. We immediately threw it in a garbage bag, prayed and burnt it in a bonfire.
>
> That evening a cool front came in and a good rain. As we cleared the debris from the fire, there were a few things that STILL remained smoldering hot! One was that movie. The Lord showed us the demonic strength of something that we thought was very small and insignificant. As soon as the movie was gone from our home, the tantrums that our young son had been throwing had ceased! To God be the glory!
>
> When my second son was an infant, he had a bowel obstruction and the doctors could not figure out what was causing it or how to help him. A few days after going through spiritual housecleaning, the Lord took me to the hall closet where I found a

book of children's stories that someone had given me. For whatever reason, I had put it away and never opened it.

I began looking through it and had a strange feeling. I finally reached the back of the book and saw that it was published by Watch Tower. This is the group that publishes the tracks and handouts for the Jehovah's Witnesses. I truly felt that this did not line up with the Word of God. I threw it in the trash and prayed. Within 30 minutes to an hour, my son began a healthy life!!

Those are some of the great stories that God has done in our home. We know that He has been faithful to show us the enemy's plans and we know that He will continue to bless us as we seek Him and ask Him—even in the little things!!

Blessings as you reach the world!

Suggestions for Dealing with an Older Child (Ages 9 to 12)

If your child is between 9 and 12 years of age, discuss the issue and explain in a little more detail the spiritual ramifications of having things that are defiled. Go through your child's room to identify these items, and then help your child research whether or not the items are things that the Lord wants them to have. Find a few Scriptures to read from *THE MESSAGE* or a children's Bible. Give your child the opportunity to get rid of any ungodly objects. If after a few days the items haven't been removed, tell the child that since he or she hasn't done so, you're going to fulfill the responsibility. You might say, "Since we are responsible for the house, we'll make decisions concerning what stays and what goes." You might offer to replace it with something better. You know your children better than anyone, so ask the Lord for a strategy that will please Him.

Suggestions for Dealing with a Teenager (Ages 13 to 18)

If your child is a teenager, do something similar to the above, but if after a few days the items haven't been removed, demand he or she get rid of the items. Explain in a quiet but firm voice that because he or she lives in your home, he or she has an obligation to you. You might say, "We want you to be happy, but until you are old and mature enough to be on your own, we expect the same respect from you that we'd expect from any adult houseguest."

If your teenager doesn't respond appropriately, have a family meeting. Both parents should sit down with the child and explain that since the teen has chosen to disrespect the house rules, an executive decision had been made. Never lose your temper. Avoid a legalistic attitude and begin your meeting in prayer, asking the Lord for wisdom and understanding. You might give the teen the opportunity to share his or her feelings. Don't interrupt! At the end, tell your child how much you appreciate his or her openness to discuss an important issue. Then explain that as parents, you are the ones who are ultimately accountable to God.

As our children became teens, we talked with them as with adults. We still remember with pride how our children did their own spiritual housecleaning. We awoke several times during those years to find sacks of video games, books and articles of clothing that they felt the Lord wanted them to discard. In some cases we didn't necessarily feel that something was that bad. But it wasn't about us; it was about their conscience and their obedience to God. We respected that and praised them for their sensitivity to the Lord.

Inappropriate Gifts Received from Others

Perhaps the most difficult thing to deal with is when someone gives your child an inappropriate gift. In this case, it's important that you don't "lower the bar" and relax the rules. Truth is truth. Never compromise truth.

Sheba Daniel sent us the following story about how a gift given by a family member caused unsettling feelings:

> After reading Derek Prince's book *Blessings or Curses You Can Choose* in 1997, I wouldn't let anything that reminded me of the devil into my house. Sometime in 2001, my cousin and her husband came to visit us one day with their baby. They brought a gift for my child—a huge Pokemon with a small Pokemon. At that time, Pokemon was very famous, but we didn't know much about it. Seeing the toy itself, however, I felt restless in my spirit. But I didn't want to offend my cousin and her family, so I kept it aside.

Since we live in a one-bedroom apartment, my cousin and her family were given the bedroom to stay for the night, and my husband, my daughter and I slept in the living room. As we were making the bed, my husband told my daughter to take that stuffed Pokemon and put it in the kitchen. When I asked him why, he said that he felt the same way as I felt, and he told me that he had no peace in his heart seeing that stuffed animal.

That night we prayed and broke that curse and told the Lord, "As soon as they leave we are going to throw this stuff out." Well, that night, my cousin's baby never slept, she was crying and crying uncontrollably and they couldn't understand why. They told me that they'd never seen their daughter cry so uncontrollably. We knew why.

The next day, after they left, we took the stuffed toys, put them in a bag and threw them into the main garbage of the building.

A few days after that, we saw a program on *The 700 Club* informing us about Pokemon, how demonic it is, and that it's actually called the "pocket monster." I thank God that the Holy Spirit made us sensitive to this and helped us deal with it.

When dealing with gifts, there are two things we would suggest: (1) don't demean the giver, talk badly of the giver or accuse the person of wrongdoing; and (2) stress the positives—the giver's generosity and thoughtfulness, for example. Also, make sure that you and your spouse are in agreement before approaching your child. You must stand together in the matter. You can trust the Holy Spirit to guide you in dealing with your children—just ask Him!

If you have children (or grandchildren or other young relatives who spend significant time in your home), take a minute now to stop and ask the Lord how to proceed in dealing with them and their possessions. Listen. Is the Lord revealing any specific objects or activities in your house (yours or the children's) that might be negatively affecting their lives? Write what you're sensing on the next page.

_____
_____
_____
_____
_____
_____
_____
_____

A Parent's Prayer of Dedication

Heavenly Father, thank You for revealing to us these things
that honor and dishonor You in our home.
We are grateful to You for giving us the discernment to identify things
that would defile our home and the wisdom to take action to protect
us. By faith, we expect to see mighty breakthroughs
as a result of our obedience to You.
Now, by the authority we have in Jesus Christ, we dedicate our home,
our possessions and our lives to You again.
We declare our freedom from the enemy's plans.
Fill our home with Your glory, Lord Jesus.
Be exalted in our house and our lives as we seek to live totally for You.
In the name of Jesus we pray.
Amen.

Notes
1. We believe that children are born with the capacity to see the spiritual as well as the natural realm. In time they tend to grow out of that ability in our society. Why? One reason is because people tend to associate anything like "seeing things that aren't there" with insanity.
2. We are not child psychologists. You may need further counsel to deal with a specific problem. If so, see your pastor or another specialist.

CHAPTER 5

Spiritual Church Cleaning

It was a small Southern church that for years had been on "spiritual life support." Sadly some churches can be in business, yet out of business, and still stay in business! This was surely one of those. They essentially existed to provide a weekly gathering place for a handful of families and to marry and bury a few folks each year.

The pastor, an evangelist at heart, was dismayed. He had tried everything he knew to resurrect the little church, yet nothing seemed to work. It was like putting makeup on a corpse. That's when he asked us to bring a team of intercessors to pray through the church property.

Why did he want us to pray through the property? He knew that only God could solve the problem. He also knew that prayer was the key to breakthrough and that God speaks best to those who speak to Him. Intercessors not only speak to God on behalf of others, but God often speaks to them on behalf of others as well.

One Thursday night we convened about 20 intercessors in the small church building. No one from the church was present, but we had been given free rein. We worshiped awhile and then began praying. At one point the Lord impressed us to read through the church's minutes. This was a church that held monthly business meetings and had written journal entries of every item of business the church had considered since it began in the early 1950s. By law they are forced to keep that record. After considerable study, the team searching through the minutes returned to the group with their report. They had discovered the following entry, in the fall of 1958:

> This past week, Jerry Jennings, our new young pastor was killed in a tragic auto accident. When Pastor Jerry died, the vision of our church died with him.

In their ignorance, without leadership at the time, the church had pronounced its own death sentence. Why? Proverbs 29:18 says, "Where there is no vision, the people perish" (*KJV*). They had voted to approve the death of the church's vision and recorded it in the legal minutes. It was so.

The Church with a Spirit of Poverty

Tom's church had grown steadily and it was now at the point that it needed to move to larger facilities. With a lot of sacrifice on the part of the people, the church was able to buy some acreage in a thriving location in the city and build a new building. On Dedication Sunday, his new building was filled with guests. Many of the members who had fallen through the cracks were back—some they hadn't seen in several years!

However, within a few months, to their surprise and disappointment, the church began to have financial difficulties. They had assumed that moving onto the new property would launch them to new levels of attendance, participation and ministry. But that wasn't the case. They were literally struggling to keep their financial heads above water.

When Pastor Tom came to us for counsel, we asked him if they had struggled financially like this before. He assured us that they hadn't. Then we asked him how they got the land on which they built their new building.

Why that question? Because we were beginning to spiritually map their situation.

Pastor Tom suddenly beamed and said, "We got this land at pennies on the dollar."

"Why was that?" we pressed.

"Well, the previous owners went bankrupt," he explained proudly, "and we picked up the property for a song."

"Perhaps so," we said, "but you got more than a piece of property. It appears to us that you also got a spirit of poverty."[1]

The previous owners had been victimized by a spirit of poverty. When they lost the land, the spirit of poverty was free to move against the new owners.

Too weird, you say?

A Church's Spirit of Jealousy

While conducting a consultation for a large denomination in the United States, one of the denominational leaders shared with me (Eddie) a problem that he was having at the small church where he was serving as interim pastor.

"When this loving church moved into their new building," he said, "all hell broke loose. People became irritable, upset, angry and even outraged. I don't have a clue how this came about, what to attribute it to or how to correct it."

I asked him where they got the property on which they built their church. He said, "It was a true blessing of the Lord. Two brothers had fought over ownership of that property for 27 years, following the death of their father. Finally, to bring peace, a judge demanded that they sell the property and split the proceeds. It was a court sale and we got a whale of a deal."

I said, "You got more than a whale of a deal on a piece of property. It sounds to me like you also purchased for yourself a spirit of jealousy, which brings division. You see, the demons that provoked those brothers for 27 years assume that they have rights to the property. Now, unless they are stopped and you purify that property and evict them, they are going to provoke you and your church members to anger and division."[2]

Failure to Properly Exercise Church Discipline

Before going to a particular church in an eastern city in the United States, we briefed our team of intercessors about why we had been asked to come and pray over the church's property. It was a large denominational church that was replete with problems of immorality, even in the highest levels of leadership. In fact, they were without a pastor at the time because their former pastor had left his wife for another woman two years before.

As part of the briefing, we discussed the proper procedure for onsite prayer: Keep your eyes open when you pray. Look for confirmation from other team members about what you are sensing the Lord may be saying. Do not hold back anything you sense the Lord say. Do not war against anything without permission from us (the leaders). Then we prayed for direction, discernment and protection.

When we arrived at the large empty facility on Thursday night, a hand-picked team of three members of the church ushered us into the pastor's study. No one else was around. We'd have the building to ourselves.

We began briefing the church's team about spiritual things like demonic strongholds that can debilitate a church and how the gifts of the Spirit described in Romans 12 and 1 Corinthians 12 are utilized in prayer. We discussed several of the ways God speaks to people through visions (e.g., by giving them a name of a person, an event or even a date or by giving them a sudden feeling of heaviness or lightness) and how the revelation God gives a team member will almost always be "in part" (see 1 Corinthians 13:9,12) because He wants us to depend entirely on Him. We explained how we listen and obey and how the pieces of information begin to fit together like the pieces of a puzzle.

We asked the church's team not to mention any details about circumstances or people in the church, unless God brought it to our attention. We always want to limit the flesh and allow the Holy Spirit to speak.

I (Alice) shared about defiled land from Psalm 106:32-38. Earlier that day, before leaving for the church, the Lord turned my attention to the book of Jude. I told the church's team that it was still unclear to me how Jude fit into the picture. Eddie invited the Holy Spirit to lead the team and prayed for darkness to be exposed and for God's light to prevail.

One vision was of a violent confrontation on a staircase leading up to the front doors; another saw the color red.

Another person described an odd-shaped number four. She thought it had to do with small children because of its childlike shape. And there were several other thoughts. With that, the pastoral and intercessory teams discussed the visions.

One of the church's team members explained that there had actually been a confrontation on the front steps of the sanctuary at one time. The front of the building (which we had not yet seen) had a long and steep staircase that led to massive doors. A pastor in the 1950s discovered that the church organist was engaged in homosexuality. One Sunday morning, the pastor angrily yanked the young man off of the organ bench, dragged him down the aisle of the church and threw him down the front steps! (Can you imagine this?) It wasn't until we intercessors were taken there later that we discovered that when the doors were opened there was a "field" of red carpet leading to the platform. We also discovered that the pastor who caused the skirmish on the front steps was later found to be an adulterer.

There are two key issues at work here:

1. *Subjective information.* When our intercessors receive "a word of knowledge" (1 Corinthians 12:8), it is subjective information. A word of knowledge is a spiritual gift whereby God grants supernatural insight and revelation. We should rarely act upon subjective information alone.

2. *Objective information.* Objective information consists of facts that have already occurred, or history that is already written, and can be validated by evidence.

A good and balanced intercessory team combines *subjective revelation* with *provable objective information* and prays to change a situation.

The number four, we discovered later, related to an almost hidden fourth floor area of the church's education facility. It was like a secret attic frequented by children and teens. When we found it, the walls had been freshly painted. The church's youth pastor had painted demonic graffiti, including many images that pertain to witchcraft that the church youth had painted on the walls (e.g., upside-down cross, broken cross, pentagram). He told us that they were a defiant and rebellious group. We prayed through the room and awaited our next step.

I (Eddie) mentioned that I sensed the Lord saying, "The answer is in the bell tower." I asked the church's team if they had a bell tower. They said that they did and that they would take us there.

But first, we walked into a baptismal dressing room where three intercessors gasped simultaneously. When we asked them what they sensed, they all expressed a feeling that sexual sin had been committed there. The shocked team concurred—it was the room used by a former pastor and a female member of the church for their sexual rendezvous.

Although I (Alice) spent most of my time interpreting the revelations others were receiving that evening, I too received several significant revelations. One concerned the church's prayer garden. The words "sexual frolic" came to mind as we stood there. The pastoral team said that the garden was known among the members through the years as a place of sexual immorality among some of the members as well as some of the staff.

We also learned that at one point, it had been in the garden that a pastor had paid off a music minister to get him to leave the church.

I read the book of Jude and, because of all we had experienced thus far, it was obvious to us why. The circumstances of the book directly related to the circumstances of the church where we were (see Jude 4 and 7). I explained to the church's team how to use the book of Jude as a prayer guide for their church. I offered prayer for further revelation and led the group in prayers of repentance on behalf of previous clergy for misleading the church.

We were almost finished when I (Eddie) remembered the bell tower. The church's team led us through the fourth floor to an area that led to the tower. Beyond that door was another flight of very narrow stairs that extended up to the belfry. The belfry was approximately 14 by 14 feet, brick, with small windows. The bell was no longer there. As soon as we stepped into the darkened belfry, I heard an odd fluttering sound. It startled me at first, because of the darkness. I began blindly reaching toward the noise near the floor and cornered and captured a poor, dehydrated, weakened pigeon. It had obviously found its way into the belfry but couldn't find its way out. As I stuck my hand through a cracked window and released it, it glided peacefully to a safe landing in the nearby tree.

It was then that we remembered, "The answer is in the bell tower." We all concluded that the pigeon was a symbol of the freedom the Lord had brought to the church that night.

At that exact moment, Alice, looking for a light switch, pulled some stage props away from a wall. When she did, there was a noticeable cool breeze that swept across the entire group. Upon examining the space behind the props, it was clear that there was no reason for the breeze—it was a solid wall. We took it as another sign of the Lord's pleasure.

The teams prayed and blessed the Lord for His revelation and for the freedom the church would now experience. As we moved back toward the pastor's study, we noticed that the heaviness in the air began to lift and even the temperature was a bit cooler.

When we entered the pastor's study at the end, everyone began to smell something amazing. The closest thing we could think of was the sweet smell of cherry-tobacco pipe smoke. It wasn't distasteful at all. Our first thought was that one of the former pastors had smoked a pipe. But later we realized that it was a supernatural incense that we smelled. It was a further sign that the Lord was blessed and the task was completed.

We can happily report that the church found a godly pastor. The former pastor left the woman he had lived with for those two years, repented and returned to his wife and kids. That was more than 10 years ago, and they are still happily married.

Lying (Sinning) to Cover Up Sin

Unfortunately, church discipline today is rarely exerted, and when it is, it is often exercised out of order. In fact, when a pastor or church staff member is dismissed because of sin, many churches never even allow the congregation to know what happened. The guilty party leaves, and then the next Sunday, an announcement is read: "Pastor John has felt his assignment here has come to a close. He has offered his resignation effective immediately so that he can find his next pastoral assignment." Baloney! The deacons and elders sat down with him and he admitted to sexual sin. Rather than repent to the church he has dishonored and resign like a man, and rather than the leadership of the church telling the truth to the members, they both lie—adding their sin to his! The result? The church is defiled and thus defeated. The answer? Spiritual church cleaning!

In Exodus 3:5, as Moses curiously approached the burning bush from which God spoke, God warned him to remove his shoes. Why? Because God said, "You're standing on holy ground." Throughout the Old Testament, references are also made to defiled land or *un*holy ground. Although many things are mentioned that can defile the land, the following five are the most common:

1. Killing innocent people (abortion, murder) (see Amos 1:13; 2 Kings 8:12; Deuteronomy 19:8-12; Isaiah 59:3-7; Luke 11:49-51)

2. Idolatry (money, possessions, idols, religious icons) (see Judges 2:1-3; Deuteronomy 12:2-3; 1 Samuel 15:23; 1 Kings 15:11-15; 16:30-33; 2 Kings 17:9-13; 2 Chronicles 15:8; Psalm 106:35-39; Ezekiel 16:29; Galatians 5:20; Colossians 3:5)

3. Sexual Immorality (adultery, fornication, prostitution, incest, rape, homosexuality, perversion) (see Jeremiah 3:1-2,9; 13:27; Ezra 9:11; Ezekiel 23:37-39; Hosea 1:2; Romans 1:18-32)

4. Broken treaties (lies, betrayal) (see Judges 2:1-3; 2 Samuel 21:1-3; Ezekiel 5:5-8)

5. Replacing the laws of God with man's laws (see Isaiah 24:5, Jeremiah 2:7-24)

Our Premise

Any place on Earth can either be holy or unholy. The determining factor is what use is made of the property. Satan has no power of his own—humankind was given dominion over the earth. The only power Satan has is given to him through humanity's sin.

And God has provided a solution. Christ died not only to reconcile us to God, but also "having made peace through the blood of his cross, by him to *reconcile all things* unto himself; by him, I say, whether they be things in earth, or things in heaven" (Colossians 1:20, *KJV*, emphasis added). Land and property can be cleansed, redeemed and reconciled to God (see Leviticus 18:24-30).

The Defilement of the Old Testament Temple

At the end of the eighth century B.C. in Jerusalem, Hezekiah's predecessors to the throne, King Ahaz and other kings before him, had defiled the Temple. Twenty-five-year-old Hezekiah, the new king of Judah and Jerusalem who had a heart to seek the Lord, took it upon himself to cleanse the Temple and make things right with the Lord so that Judah and Jerusalem could again receive God's blessings and protection.

Hezekiah Purifies the Temple
Take another look at 2 Chronicles 29:1-19.

- *What was the problem?* The Temple had been defiled (see v. 5). Church buildings can be defiled just as the Temple was defiled. The Assyrians, the enemies of God's people, defeated Judah, carrying off women and children as captives (see v. 9). When we open our churches to Satan through sin and defiled objects, family members can be "carried off" and taken captive by satanic forces. Churches grow weak because God removes His presence and, thus, His blessings.

- *How did the Temple become defiled?* The "fathers," former kings and Hezekiah's predecessors to the throne, had turned away from the Lord, disobeyed the Lord's commands to maintain Temple worship with the order the Lord had laid out in the Law of Moses, and had defiled the Temple with abominable objects (see vv. 6-7).

- *What steps were taken to correct the problem?* First, Hezekiah renewed the covenant, or commitment, with the Lord (see v. 10). Then, under Hezekiah's direction, the priests consecrated and purified themselves (see v. 15). They also purified the temple (see v. 15) by removing everything unclean from the Temple (see v. 16). Finally, the priests put back utensils that God commanded them to keep there (see vv. 18-19). When we purify our lives, confessing our sins, repenting of and reversing our sinful activities, and removing from our churches things that displease the Lord, the favor of God can return to our lives so that we experience His peace and blessings.

• *What was the result?* God was pleased and His favor returned to
Judah and Jerusalem under Hezekiah. This is implied by verse
2: "He did what was right in the eyes of the LORD" (*NIV*).

Idol Feasts and the Lord's Supper
Read 1 Corinthians 10:14-33.

• *What was the problem?* Corinth was an idolatrous city. Worshipers
of demons offered sacrificial animals to their gods. As soon as
the sacrifice was complete, they would carry the carcass into the
temple meat market and sell it to people on the streets. Paul
maintained that eating this meat wasn't a problem unless it
caused others to stumble. But there were other Christians who
actually participated in the rituals and ate at the temple tables
with the heathens (see Romans 8). This prompted Paul's corrective word to Corinthian believers not to frequent heathen
temples and eat at their ceremonial tables, and then at the
same time participate in the Lord's Supper (Communion) (see
1 Corinthians 10:18-22).

• *Why was this a problem?* Paul explained to the Corinthian believers that they actually participated with demons when they
partook of the food that had been dedicated to the idols (see
vv. 18-20). Likewise, if we have items or places in our churches
that relate to demonic forces or that have been defiled by sin,
then we become unwitting participants with demonic forces
attached to those defiled objects or places.

• *What were the results?* This results in the Lord's jealousy being
aroused over His people. Believe us, you don't want to be on
the receiving end of God's jealousy and anger. Often when the
Lord was angry with the Israelites, He turned them over to
trouble, calamity and defeat at the hands of their enemies.
Consider the following passage in Ezra 9:10-11:

> But now, O our God, what can we say after this? For we
> have disregarded the commands you gave through your

servants the prophets when you said: "The land you are
entering to possess is a land polluted by the corruption of
its peoples. By their detestable practices they have filled it
with their impurity from one end to the other" (*NIV*).

This passage makes it clear that the land of Canaan, the
Promised Land, had been polluted and defiled by the sins of
the Canaanites and then later by the Israelites. Land on which
our homes or churches sit can be defiled by the sins of previous occupants or by our own sins.

• *What did this produce?* This produced the following results:

* *Chain-reaction sin.* Pastoral leaders are gatekeepers
(see John 10:1-3; Acts 20:28). Gatekeepers open and
close the gates to people and entities approaching
the city. In the case of a pastor, what he allows into
his own life, he is in effect allowing into the flock,
the church membership. When he sins and his sin
is not dealt with properly, a chain reaction often
occurs, just as sin's tendencies are passed to the
third and four generations from fathers to sons. It
is not uncommon that young men and weak
Christians fall into sexual sin as a result of a pastor's (spiritual father's) sins. This is what happened
in the large denominational church described earlier in this chapter.

* *Public loss of confidence.* Once a church or congregation has been defiled by the misdeeds of leadership,
it loses its influence in the community. First the
church stops following its appointed leader.
Eventually the community no longer holds the
church and its leadership in high regard. The congregation becomes known by the sins of their leader
more so than anything else they may have done.

* *Spiritual powerlessness.* When sin has been committed in the church and left hidden by leadership, the first one who stops attending the services is the Holy Spirit. He is grieved and no longer manifests His presence.

* *Atmospheric interference.* Oddly, spiritually discerning, godly people will attend one service and be unconsciously turned off. They may not even know why. They simply won't be back. They sensed something wrong and they were unable to attach confidence to the church. This "sense" can sometimes be traced to past or current sin by the church leadership.

* *Relational difficulties.* When the net is broken, the fish escape. When relational problems are left unresolved in the Body of Christ, the blessings are lost. We are ministers of reconciliation (see 2 Corinthians 5:18-19). We are to make restitution where necessary. Often we are trying to convince the world to be reconciled to God and they question us in their response by saying, "Why would I want to be reconciled to God, when you aren't even willing to be reconciled to one another?" When we fail to maintain reconciliation, we cause cracks to form in the foundations of the Church, and relationships erode.

* *Lack of discernment; spiritual blindness.* When we fail to act upon the things that God reveals to us, we will get to a place where He no longer speaks. Light (spiritual discernment and revelation) is given where light is received. This is true of churches as well as individuals.

These are some of the ways a church's building and property become defiled, its fellowship spiritually crippled, and its ministries compromised.

What to Do If You Know of a Church with This Problem

If you are the pastor of a church with any of these problems, you have a very difficult job ahead of you. This is especially true if it relates to the sins, or failings, of previous pastors. Why? It may appear that you are simply jealous or that you are pointing to their failures to make yourself look good.

In this position, it's crucial for you to hear the heart of Christ. Remember to balance mercy with justice. It is helpful to have one or more associates that you can partner with in the process. However, they should be well selected, because you will be discussing sensitive things that are emotionally charged.

One pastor we love dearly moved too quickly in a situation of this sort and an elderly church couple, who had been in the church for decades, felt threatened, causing the pastor, his family and church great harm. You will need the mind of Christ. We suggest you move cautiously and carefully. What the enemy has taken years to accomplish doesn't have to be overturned overnight. Move according to God's timetable.

Prayer and fasting should precede any corrective action. It's usually best made with a small group of committed Christians who are mature enough to deal with these matters. We realize, however, that there are also times when a pastor has to make the move alone, privately.

My (Eddie's) father was once the new pastor of a church that had suffered a church split years before he came. When he found out about it, he scheduled a Sunday evening for his entire congregation to attend the other church's evening service. We entered the other church's auditorium, filled the empty seats and stood around the walls, as my dad walked to the front and asked permission to speak. The gracious host pastor handed him the microphone. My preacher daddy apologized for the actions that had been taken by his church years before he came to pastor it, actions that had helped bring about the church split. The reconciliation between the churches was a huge breakthrough for the city. Dad and the pastor became friends, and the churches are at peace with each other to this day.

We've seen pastors assemble a small group of leaders to purify church property. They've used different procedures, as led by the Holy

Spirit. We call these "prophetic acts" because they are symbolic of the spiritual truths that are being applied. Here are a few things we've observed:

1. Prayers of repentance for previous sins are followed by prayers of replacement (e.g., "Lord, cleanse us from the sin of sexual promiscuity and make us a people of sexual purity").

2. Oil is dabbed above the doors and windows of the building as each room is dedicated to the Lord.

3. A covenant of love, stating the purpose of the church, is written and the members sign it into the church's legal records.

4. Entire congregations have a night of dedication, signing a document of commitment to God. These services may have repentance, replacement prayers, and prayers of purification and purpose.

5. Groups gather at the four corners of the property and corporately read passages of Scripture and pray prayers of dedication.

6. The building or property is marched around seven times.

7. Scripture is printed, folded or rolled up and inserted into a short piece of half-inch PVC pipe with a cap on each end. One of those pipes is driven into the ground at each of the four corners of the property. Oil or wine is poured on each to symbolize purification and dedication.

8. Declarations renouncing the sins—breaking contracts and legal agreements with demons and darkness—and evicting any spirits that are associated presently with the property are read aloud. Then the property is dedicated to the Lord, and freedom is pronounced.

This isn't an exhaustive list, but it includes procedures that have proven to be powerful. Seek the Lord on behalf of your church and/or church property and ask Him how best to cleanse and dedicate it. Ask Him to speak to you through the Word, through trusted spiritual leaders and through intercessors.

If you are a member of a church that you think needs spiritual cleaning, we suggest that you ponder the need in your heart. Don't share it with anyone, unless he or she is the one who will be directly responsible for correcting the problem (e.g., the pastor). And *pray*. We often say, "Diagnosis doesn't necessarily mean assignment." Just because you have diagnosed a church problem, it doesn't mean you have the assignment to fix it. Prayer is powerful and effective. There may be nothing more for you to do other than pray.

When you feel you have sufficient verifiable information, pray about the right time to bring it to your pastor's attention. When the time comes, make an appointment to meet with your pastor privately. Be prepared to present your evidence, and be accompanied by witnesses if possible. Most important, be gentle and humble. Leave the matter with the pastor. He or she is ultimately responsible before God once he or she knows the details.

If you are not a member of the church that you know has been defiled, the handling of the problem depends on the situation. We'll give you two examples.

One day, I (Eddie) received a call from one of our faithful and godly church members. She told me about a large nearby church with more than 2,000 members, where she had once been a member. A reliable source had reported to her that this church had been infiltrated by a coven of witches. She went on to describe the situation, including the sacrificing of a cat in the church's prayer room. Her source seemed credible.

The question was what I should do about the situation. I wasn't a member of the church. I was a pastor of another church in the same area. I understood that my mentioning the problem to the pastor could be considered an accusation against him and his people. And I would never want that. So I went to another pastor on our church staff, one who had impeccable credentials, and asked if he would go with me to share what I had learned with the other pastor. He agreed, so I made an appointment with the pastor of this large church.

We were cordially received in an elegant office and invited to be seated. I'm sure my heart was beating so strongly that it could be seen through my shirt!

"What brings you fellows here today?" the unsuspecting pastor asked.

I explained that we had good reason to believe that his church had been infiltrated by witches at the highest levels and that a ceremony had been conducted in their prayer room that included the sacrificing of a cat. Frankly, I was prepared for an outburst of disbelief. Instead, he furrowed his brow and quietly said, "Excuse me, gentlemen, I'll be back in a moment." He then left us sitting alone. We looked at each other inquisitively. *What could he possibly be about to do?*

Moments later he returned, followed by six or seven of his fellow staff pastors. "Tell them what you told me," he urged. I did.

Then, one by one, they began to share how the Lord started exposing the infiltrators several months before. Three or four of the infiltrators had been removed from top leadership positions. Several were asked to leave the adult choir. The pastoral staff thanked us for coming by to confirm their experiences. Then they asked if we would go with them to their prayer room for a time of purification. We did.

A different situation called for a different solution. This time we were visiting a foreign country. As we stepped off the plane, we were met by the missionary who would be our host for the next several days. He was an American missionary in this major foreign city. On the way to his house, he explained how expensive property was and how fortunate they were to have their place of worship.

"Where do you meet?" we asked.

"We meet in the [he named the building]. It's an ideal worship facility. And we almost missed it. You see, another church had it rented on Sunday mornings. So the owner offered us Friday nights. But I did some investigative work and found out how much the other church was paying. I offered the owner more, and he immediately bumped them to Friday night and gave us prime time on Sunday morning. Amazing, isn't it?"

After a few minutes of driving, I (Eddie) said, "Pastor, what do we have planned for tonight?"

"Nothing at all—you can rest. Why?"

"We'd like to attend church."

"Church? What church?" he asked puzzled.

"The church that meets on Friday night," I explained.

"Why on earth would you want to attend *that* church?" he asked.

"Pastor, we'd like to attend that church to give you the opportunity to repent to them for taking their worship time. For if you think we are going to stay in your country and minister in your church with this sin hanging over your head, you are sadly mistaken. We'll catch the next plane home."

Needless to say, he was shocked—and convicted. After a few moments of thoughtful deliberation, he humbly agreed.

That night we went to the church, and after we had sat for a few moments, I was able to get the pastor's attention. I said to him, "Pastor, my name is Eddie. I'm from the United States. I have with me the pastor of the church that meets in this facility on Sunday mornings. He is the one who took your Sunday-morning worship time from you. He is here to repent publicly to you and your people for doing that. Would you allow us two or three minutes of your time tonight?"

He graciously agreed. And when the time came, he introduced me. I then introduced my host pastor. He stood before the people and sincerely and tearfully repented to them for the backhanded way he had treated them. When he finished, I asked, "People, will you forgive the pastor for what he has done to you?" It was a powerful experience that night to be a part of the healing of two churches.

What Should You Expect?

We think you should expect a supernatural response. In the case of the two churches described in the last story, members of both congregations began to meet together for picnics in city parks. They merged some of their ministries and the pastors preached in each other's pulpits in the months that followed. And over the next two years, both churches tripled in size!

What does God expect? Mark 11:15-17 states, "On reaching Jerusalem, Jesus entered the temple area and began driving out those who were buying and selling there. He overturned the tables of the money changers and the benches of those selling doves, and would not allow anyone to carry merchandise through the temple courts. And as he taught them, he said, 'Is it not written: "My house will be called a house of prayer for all nations"? But you have made it "a den of robbers."'"

What does this passage reveal about Jesus' zeal for the house of God? Was He calm and peaceful about it? No! We serve a passionate God who is, as we've noted, jealous for His name's sake and for the pure-hearted devotion of His people. Some things in our churches and on our church property might not seem like sin but might be standing in the way of undistracted worship and of our entering into the presence of God. As these verses reveal, God will not tolerate the competition!

Let's follow Jesus' example in our churches, our homes, and in our hearts—and wherever we have authority to cleanse and purify a place for His glory. Let's make it our mission to keep His church clean, to keep it as He desires: *a house of prayer for all nations.*

Notes
1. Not every piece of property bought from a bankruptcy sale has a demonic attachment. Often it is determined by the ongoing sin that is associated with the property.
2. Not every piece of property bought at a court-ordered sale has a demonic attachment or would be considered defiled land. Learning the facts of the case along with unusual activities would be a more accurate way to determine the problem.

CHAPTER 6

Work, Other People's Property, and Loved Ones

Ever felt "slimed" at work—not necessarily by a person, but by the environment itself? Ever wondered why it's hard to concentrate, to communicate, why profits are down, and what to do about profanity, pornography or other offensive material openly displayed in the break room? What's the spiritual climate of your workplace? If it's your own business or if you work from your home, you can easily cleanse your work environment of past sins and lingering foul spirits. But what do you do when you don't have that authority? How can you shed light on a dark atmosphere when it's not your business or your building?

What about other people's property? What can you do when your neighbor's behavior is an abomination to the whole street or when you rent a "haunted" hotel room? What kind of action can you take if another person's possessions or property manifest some kind of demonic power that directly affects your life?

And what about your loved ones? What if an unsaved family member moves into your home and brings with them spiritual roommates of a demonic nature? Or if a friend or relative gives you or your child a gift that's spiritually offensive?

Hard questions to answer, but the good news is that even difficult situations such as these can be solved with some simple spiritual housecleaning know-how, humility and a heart of faith. The following stories illustrate strategies for dealing with the demonic in your workplace, on other people's property and with your loved ones who don't know any better. But first let's begin with Zacchaeus, a little man in the Bible who, upon his encounter with Christ, took immediate action to clean up his act—and his business!

Read Luke 19:1-9. When Zacchaeus encountered Christ, what was his response?

_____

_____

_____

_____

_____

_____

_____

What did he do to rectify his bad business practices?

_____

_____

_____

_____

_____

_____

What did Jesus say to Zacchaeus and his *entire household* at that moment?

_____

_____

_____

_____

_____

_____

_____

Wow! Can you imagine giving half of your possessions to the poor and paying back *four times over* anyone you'd cheated? Imagine the results of such an act of repentance. By fully trusting God and making right his wrongs, Zacchaeus may have cut off massive demonic forces that were operating in his work and life.

Before going any further, take a moment to examine your own work ethic. Before cleansing the environment we work in, we first must evaluate the heart that we work *from*. Is your heart pure and undefiled, or does it need a good washing before going up against the demons in the office? Are you giving your boss and your company 100 percent of your best? Have you stayed free from a legalistic and judgmental attitude at work?

Write out Psalm 139:23-24 and Matthew 5:8. What do these verses say about the importance of first having a heart that's clean before God?

_____

_____

_____

_____

_____

_____

_____

Prayer Changes Everything!

One woman's courage to wield spiritual authority at work led to her promotion and the company's prosperity. She writes:

> I knew it was time to begin looking for a new job. After an interview with this company, I was offered the position. I had a strong feeling that this was the Lord's will. It seemed like just another chapter in my book of life.
>
> By the end of the first day, I sensed some things very out of order. I went into the break room to heat up some lunch and felt like I had slime all over me. When I turned around to leave, I saw an array of pictures of topless women. I wondered what I had gotten myself into. I knew that this would have to go or else I would have to go. Knowing that this job was God's will, the choice was obvious. I began to pray against lust, pornography, perversion and anything else I felt the Lord was showing me.

After a couple of weeks, I felt a strange and unwarranted resentment from the female office manager that I did not understand at first. As the days progressed I increasingly felt that something was not right with this lady. Things didn't seem to add up with her. She was often absent, which she explained was because she was pregnant and having a difficult time. I could not bring myself to believe that. I began to pray that every hidden thing would be brought to the light. I prayed against witchcraft and deception. In my mind I did not understand why I would pray these things, but I felt compelled to pray them.

One day I was bored, so I asked my boss if I could reconcile the bank accounts—which was the office manager's job, but she was not there. Halfway through the process I realized that there was a check missing that was written for a rather sizable amount. My boss called the bank and they said the check had been written to the office manager. I then worked for 3 days searching the records without her knowing about it. I discovered that she had embezzled almost $20,000 from the company. Everything that was hidden was indeed brought to the light.

She lost her job and I was given her position with a rather nice raise. I still knew I needed to pray through the building and get rid of the demonic activity that I could sense there, but it was difficult to do that while at work. I prayed the Lord would give me a time when I could be alone in the building to do spiritual cleaning.

One day my boss came to me and said the cleaning lady had quit. I offered to clean on the weekends as a part-time job. He liked that idea and gave me a key to the building, which was just what I needed. I smiled as I knew I would have the building all to myself and could clean it both physically and spiritually.

I came in that weekend and put on some praise music and began with the lunch room. I prayed through all the offices and through the whole building. After only two weeks of praying, the pictures on the wall in the break room were taken down. I never had to say a word. I praised the Lord and kept pressing in and praying through the building. I began to throw away magazines and catalogs that had occult articles and items in them. I threw away "adult" newspapers every week until they disappeared altogether.

As I first began to take over the accounts as the new office manager, I noticed that we had only enough money to barely get by. I knew that the company had to be blessed in order for me to be blessed. I would lay hands on the checks as I printed them, calling in the blessings and commanding the evil to leave. After one year, our sales had doubled and we had over $100,000 in the bank, which is good for a small company. The owners of the company recognize that the blessing they are experiencing is because of the Lord's hand.

We have had an abundance of work when other shops are laying people off. The entire atmosphere has changed, and it is now both blessed and a blessing. Some people have left, which I know was God's way of purifying, and others have come in that I sense are a link in God's plan for the future of the company. It's a joy to go to work where I know it's my ministry field. I believe that we do not have to settle for the atmosphere that we work in, but we can create change if we are diligent to pray, be patient, stay humble and spiritually cleanse our workplace. Greater indeed is He that is in us, than he that is in the world. Change can be a very good thing and the effect can be seen by those around, even if they do not understand the spiritual aspect. We do understand and know who to give the glory to.

What are the positives and negatives of your work environment?

_____

_____

_____

_____

_____

_____

_____

_____

What can you do to cleanse your workplace and make it a place of light, a place rich with the presence of God? (Consider showing up early and quietly prayer-walking the offices, praying during your noon lunch break, beginning a prayer meeting at lunch or fasting for a season for breakthrough.)

_____

_____

_____

_____

_____

A Coworker Opens the Door to Spiritual Oppression

In our multicultural and religiously diverse society, you never know what kinds of spiritual activities your coworkers are involved in. Janell Price shared with us the following story of how a spirit of heaviness (depression) came upon her when she allowed an officemate to "read her cards":

> About 30 years ago, I took a temporary secretarial job in a small insurance office. Every work day, I ate lunch with one of the lady agents in her office—we were the only two females there. One day, she took out a pack of cards and casually began to read my cards. I don't remember that she asked or that I said yes or no. I was so ignorant I didn't know what tarot cards were.[1] One of the things she foretold for me happened later that day. It didn't make me a believer in the occult and I never had another encounter with the occult. But that wasn't because I knew it was of the enemy or against God's law. I was a born-again Christian who knew very little of the Scriptures.
>
> Sometime later, my husband and I were filled with the Holy Spirit and began going to a charismatic church. Because I was suffering from constant severe depression, I made an appointment with the pastor (Judson Barnwell, then of New Testament Baptist Church, Houston, Texas, now residing in heaven). The heaviness I felt made life seem unbearable. Thoughts of suicide came to my

mind. I had a wonderful husband and two beautiful children, but there was no joy in my life.

Following an opening prayer by Pastor Judson in his office, God gave him a picture in his mind of my encounter with the coworker and her tarot cards. He described to me what he was seeing and showed me in the Scriptures that I had violated God's law and invited the enemy into my life. Upon hearing the truth, I took responsibility for what I had done, even though I had done it in ignorance. I was sorrowful about grieving God and I repented. Pastor Judson then took authority over the spirit of heaviness and it left. As I came out of the church building, I noticed that the sun was shining and I felt that life was good. The deliverance was complete and permanent.

In my case, the cleansing of my spiritual house—the one my spirit and soul live in, the one the Holy Spirit lives in—came before the cleansing of my physical house. But the principle was the same: knowing God's truth, lining up with it, and ridding myself of vile things.

It was a life-changing lesson for me. I was struck by how devastating the results of my one encounter with fortunetelling had been, even though I had not sought it out and hadn't put faith in it. After I returned home from my deliverance appointment, my husband and I read the Scriptures related to the occult and forbidden objects and went through everything in our home, throwing out anything that was expressly forbidden or doubtful. We gave special attention to our children's possessions, aware of the devastation that can come from so-called innocent involvement. We have continued to stay vigilant from that day to this, having nothing to do with forbidden things. God has been faithful. The spirit of heaviness has not returned (see Isaiah 61:3).

What Do You Do When It's Not Your Property?

As with church property, demons can inhabit a home, business, or any other kind of land or facility and can continue to wreak havoc there if not properly dealt with.

An apartment manager in Houston told us, "I always dread to see a young happy couple move into Apartment 321."

"Why's that?" we queried.

"Every couple that moves into that apartment, no matter the condition of their relationship when they move in, is divorced within a year," she said.

Division lingered in that apartment. An infestation of ants or roaches is bad. An infestation of evil spirits is worse. As soon as these demons of division did their work on one couple, another unsuspecting couple would move in.

Jack York, a different manager, shares how he took his authority in Christ, along with the spiritual housecleaning tools he had learned, to implement *real* home improvement on the property he managed:

> I have cleaned house several times and I believe that it all stemmed from hearing Alice speak at a convention here in 1996. Since then I have read most of your books at least twice.
>
> After the conference where Alice had asked us to allow God to show us anything in our homes that wasn't right, I went home and removed everything that God told me to remove. From that time, I prayed through my apartment, asking God to show me anything that wasn't right. I also anointed all the entrances and I went outside and prayed over all things that I had authority over. I lived in that neighborhood for over eight years and NEVER had my car broken into or my apartment touched. Others in the neighborhood had break-ins in both vehicles and residences.
>
> Since that time I have moved to another location. As I was given charge of the grounds to mow and keep clean, I went and prayed over the property, and even staked it on the four corners of the compass with a *Red Book* Bible and a cross, claiming the territory for God. The house itself, which used to be a roadhouse, I have prayed over numerous times and have swept it clean. Again when we moved in, I asked God if there was anything in all I possessed that was not right. He had me throw out several hundred dollars worth of stuff that wasn't right for a

man of God to have. Since that time, two years ago, the house has been at peace. Even when other homes in the neighborhood were broken into by burglars, ours was untouched.

Even when cleaned, stuff can get tracked in or allowed in through the phone lines, TV or PC, but when the Holy Spirit brings it to mind, I clean through again and we're at peace. I believe that the enemies of God realize whose property this is and veer away.

Dealing with Employee Possessions on Your Property

Bob Williams (not his real name) owns a large furniture manufacturing plant in North Carolina. His wife, Loraine, is a wonderful Christian. Bob, now a vibrant Christian, was unsaved when Loraine convinced him to have a team of intercessors come and pray through their business. She told him that it would be good to have the business blessed and to see if the Lord would show the prayer team anything that displeased Him. Bob agreed.

On Thursday night of that week, after business hours and all the employees had gone home, we showed up with our team of intercessors. We first prayed and asked the Holy Spirit to be honored and blessed in this business. Then we explained to Bob and Loraine that we were going to start at the receptionist's desk and visually investigate the wall hangings, décor and other things in sight. Then we would pray for discernment regarding the spiritual atmosphere of each employee space.

Perhaps because of Loraine's influence, the offices were fairly clean. Bob was amazed when a couple of the intercessors, hearing from God, began to tell him about some of his former employees. Hearing them describe an affair between two of his former employees "blew him away." The story was true, but Bob was the only one who could have known it. God often shares His secrets with intercessors so that they can pray properly. Information is the fuel of intercession, so God typically speaks to those who speak to Him.

When the team moved into the furniture construction area, it was another story. Several of the men had girlie calendars hanging on the walls of their work spaces. The intercessors (mostly ladies) were offended by the sight of them. We suggested to Bob that the calendars with the nude photos dishonored the Lord and were a bad testimony for his business.

Bob honored the team's instruction and immediately charged into each space, pulled the offensive calendars off the walls and took them to the trash dumpster! Great, huh?

Not so fast.

You see, the next morning when the employees arrived at work and noticed their missing calendars, they lined up at Bob's door to ask him who had been meddling with their stuff. Bob explained that the calendars were inappropriate and that he had removed them. There was quite a bit of tension, which brought Bob to say, "Guys, I'll give each of you some money so that you can go buy a *suitable* calendar for your wall"— which he did.

If you are a business owner, consider doing what Bob and Loraine did and bring in a team to pray through your business. You are responsible for the spiritual atmosphere in your company. You might find that it would settle some of your employee and financial problems.

However, *don't* do what Bob did and destroy property that belongs to someone else. It's true that the men didn't own their workspaces and that, in a legal sense, Bob had the right to do what he did. However, there is a better way. What Bob should have done was call a meeting of the employees to explain to them that he had decided that the calendars would have to go, and why. Then he could have given his employees 24 hours to remove or replace the calendars, or he could have offered to buy them new calendars. In either case, he could then thank them for their cooperation. This would have shown them respect, would have allowed them to do the right thing and would have enabled them to save face in the process.

Dealing with a Family Member Who Defiles Your Home

Sometimes, in tough situations, tough love is required. One woman shared with us the following story about how her mother defiled her home:

I was born on an island and until the age of 15, I lived with my parents and five other siblings. My dad was going to move to another island to work, and we were moving with him. But my mother could not handle the move, so she moved back home. We children were left with Dad.

Over the years, mother would visit us in the U.S., stay with each of us for a while and then go back home. I knew as a child that my mother was very superstitious. She was always doing some kind of ritual, but I thought that that was just a thing of the past. I did not realize that my mother never left her work of witchcraft and superstitious beliefs.

Not too long ago, my mother was coming to visit me and I remember being excited, getting a room ready for her, making sure everything was in order for her. I was not very happy with my job at the time and had discussed with my mother how evil I thought the people were. I told her all the mean things they would do to me on my job. So she suggested that I write each of these individual's name on a piece of paper, and then we were going to cut them in little pieces with scissors, while we said, "So and so, let evil return to evil." Sadly, I fell into my mother's tricks and witchery. It was soon after this episode that I quit my job. However, I thought how strange it was that I had put up with my unhappy job for so long and, yet, no sooner had my mother come, that I would quit my job so fast. But then I did not think about it anymore.

Before this episode, my mother told me that she was going to fix a bath for me that consisted of coffee, sugar and honey. As not to disrespect her, I reluctantly agreed. I actually did not bathe in that awful colored bath water but discarded it. There was also another ritual that she convinced me to participate in. It had to do with lighting a candle and then swaying the lit candle all around my body and saying something that I cannot recall exactly. Not once did she use the name of Jesus.

Even though I reluctantly agreed with my mother to do these rituals, I had a very strong objection to how she adored the moon—especially a full moon. We would be sitting outside on the patio taking in the lovely breeze, and she would tell me that I needed to talk to the moon and tell the moon how lovely she is and that I love her, and so on. I strongly objected to this, so I would tell her, "No, you are not supposed to adore the moon. It is very unacceptable to the Lord God."

And another thing that I could not stand was when she burned incense in the house. I could not stand the smell. So I asked her to please not do it in the house. So my mom would go into the garage to burn incense and conduct her rituals. I started to notice that my mother's facial features would change during her rituals and that she would tie her hair up like someone going to war. I tried very hard to be nice and respectful to her, but I could see her facial features change, her demeanor change and her attitude change. I realized that she was out of control doing her witchcraft when I was at work.

During my mom's stay, I became very restless—normally I'm a busy person. I was confused and unable to concentrate, and I was getting out of control myself. As soon as I would get home from work, I would become very restless. Something was wrong with me, but I could not pinpoint what it was.

Instead of going home, many days I would go to the stores. I felt in my spirit that something was not right at home. My mother would sit in a chair and watch my every move. I could feel an energy drawing and pulling me to her. I felt this energy coming from her that wanted to control me, and I was fighting it within me.

One night, as my mother and I were sitting in the garage, she said, "There is someone out there. Do you hear it?" And I could hear the wind blowing furiously, rattling the garage doors. Even though I felt it was odd, I said, "Oh, Mother, there's no one out there! See?" And I went to the front door and opened it so that she could be at ease. As strange as this may sound, I believe demons came in my house when I opened the front door. When I went to bed that night, demons were rattling my bed frame, causing me a lot of fear.

I was becoming increasingly restless and confused and I was unable to sleep well. Besides the fact that I felt hopeless, helpless and spiritually defeated, all peace and joy in the Lord had left me.

One night while my mother was gone with one of my siblings, the Holy Spirit showed me that it was my mother who brought demonic spirits into my house. As soon as she returned, I unwisely confronted her, lashed out and scolded her. I rebuked her, insisting that I wanted her demons out of my house. I told her that witchcraft was an abomination to God.

I called my family to tell them that if they did not get Mother out of my house, I was going to the hospital, for she had brought me to the breaking point. After hours of rebuking and commanding demons to leave my house, a calm peace came upon me. That's when I realized for sure that my mother had my house full of demons. I fell asleep that night and slept well for the first time in a very long time.

When I came home from work the next day, my mother was there. I threatened my siblings to get her out of my house. They finally came and picked her up. When I gained my composure, I just couldn't believe this was happening to me. After all, I had been a born-again Christian for so long. I always would recite the Scripture that no weapon formed against me shall prosper, because greater is He that is in me than he that is in the world. But in reality, I had let my guard down. It's tragic that I had to deal with my own mother, who was involved in occult practices.

As I dug my heels in my Bible, seeking God, the Holy Spirit revealed to me that my sorcerer mother had brought the demons inside the house with her witchcraft. But I wasn't innocent, because I had participated in my mother's rituals, compromising and neglecting my relationship with Jesus. I prayed to God, repenting for my sin like I had never done before. And the Lord revealed so much truth to me. Daily, my peace returned, my joy returned, and my strength returned. God's mercy and grace were with me to overcome this terrible experience. The Holy Spirit brought to light and understanding the spiritual world that I had never realized was there before.

My greatest regret is that I didn't handle my mother in a loving way, because I was scared. I didn't understand at the time what was happening to me. I should have controlled my anger.

When I felt spiritually stronger, about four months later, I had the courage to go visit my sister's house to say goodbye to my mother, who was leaving the States to go back to the islands. I asked her to forgive me for the way I had handled the situation. I don't know if she has, but I pray God will have mercy on her soul.

While this woman could not force her mother to change, she could have (and eventually did) enforce the rules of her home—and forced anyone who would not abide by those rules to leave. You have spiritual authority over your home; therefore, you have the right to ask any adult who defiles your home to leave. The approach might vary from situation to situation, but your first step should always be *prayer*, seeking God for guidance and discernment. You might seek another trusted believer to pray both for and with you. Respect, gentleness and graciousness should be used whenever possible when dealing with loved ones (especially older relatives). Sometimes, however, if the other person is belligerent or endangering the safety of your family, swift and bold (but still God-honoring) action is a must. Be sure to go through your home and scour it thoroughly with prayer and praise, throwing out any defiled objects that your former roommate or houseguest might have left behind.

Note

1. The Tarot is a set of cards displaying allegorical symbols. Originally used as playing cards, they later came to be used for divination—witchcraft. The cards are divided into Major and Minor Arcana and are used for spiritual, esoteric, psychological, occult and/or divinatory purposes.

CHAPTER 7

Spiritual Housecleaning Wisdom and Warnings

Welcome! You cannot imagine how pleased we are to see that you've arrived at chapter 7. Statistics show that of all the people who buy and begin to read Christian books, only a small percentage complete them. You are one of those special few who have fought your way through life's distractions and set aside the time to read this far. You've certainly proved your commitment to bring God glory through personal freedom for both you and your family.

We minister around the world in seminars, conferences and other settings. But some of our most favorite and fruitful ministry was when we served as pastors. Perhaps that is because we love people and enjoy seeing them move to new levels of spiritual maturity. So we want this final chapter to be a bit more pastoral. If we were your pastors, these are 12 things we would encourage you to keep in mind when conducting spiritual housecleaning or dealing with darkness on any level.

1. Remember Who You Are

If you are born again, you are God's child. Christ is in you, and you are in Christ. God has made you the righteousness of Christ. You don't *do right* in order to *become* righteous. You *do right* because you *are righteous*! (See 2 Corinthians 5:21.)

2. Recognize Your Position

Christ has already won the war against the devil and his demons. Satan's utter eternal defeat is an absolute accomplished fact. Jesus defeated and disarmed him at Calvary. Satan's only two remaining weapons are *lies* and *deception*. Our role at this point is nothing more than a mopping-up exercise. When one army defeats another, the war is over. However, there often remain raids to perform, skirmishes to engage in, and prisoners to take as that victory is enforced. Today, we are enforcing the victory that Christ won at Calvary.

3. Understand Your Rights
You have all the rights of an ambassador. Earth is no longer your true home. Your home is in heaven. You are here on temporary duty for your King. As an ambassador, you can demand what your King is demanding, say what your King is saying and announce proclamations your King has made.

4. Always Operate from a Position of Victory!
Don't operate defensively; operate offensively. Don't be a responder; be an initiator. Run to the battle, not from the battle. The devil's gates will not be able to withstand you!

5. Fear Not
Demons are more afraid of you than you could ever be of them. When they see you, they see Christ's glorious life in you, and they are stricken with fear. When you are walking in obedience, filled with His Holy Spirit, they are no match at all for you. Your greatest temptation will most likely be to *fear* them. The enemy takes particular pride in seeing us afraid. If you don't fall for that trick, he'll reverse his tactics and tempt you with spiritual pride.

6. Avoid Pride
Never forget that the victories you've had in Christ were His victories. Don't focus on what you've done. Remain focused on who Christ is and what He's done for you, in you and through you. This is the key to maintaining victory.

7. Avoid Superstition
Many Christians who begin to understand the things we've written about in this book become "demon-conscious" and superstitious, and draw faulty conclusions about things. Always remember the following:

- *There are a limited number of demons.* Even if a door has been left open, it doesn't necessarily follow that a demon has taken advantage of it any more than if you leave the door of your house open, a mosquito will *always* fly in.

- *Satan and his demons are not omnipresent.* They can only be in one place at a time. Don't credit them with more than they deserve.

8. Avoid Ritualism

If you submit to superstition, you'll likely give in to ritualism. Spiritual life is a result of relationship—not rituals. There are no silver bullets or magic words when it comes to spiritual warfare. Every assignment and encounter is unique. In every case, we must depend entirely upon the Holy Spirit.

Sure, we can learn from the experiences of others—both from their successes and from their failures. That's exactly why we wrote this book. But we are not to attempt to duplicate what they did. Listen to the Holy Spirit before, during and following any spiritual-warfare task. We take orders from Jesus, the Lord of Host and the Captain of heaven's army!

9. Don't Become a Legalistic and Judgmental Christian

Those who fall into *ritualism* succumb to *legalism* and are useless in the kingdom of God. Legalistic Christians view themselves as God's police force and rarely win anyone to Christ. No one wants to even be around them, much less be like them. You may have received new, fresh revelation as you've been reading this book. Don't mistake that for spiritual maturity. Maturity is not an accumulation of spiritual knowledge, a collection of memorized Scriptures or an understanding of principles. Spiritual maturity is Christ's likeness—God's love and grace operating in us.

Scripture warns us not to judge other men's servants. It's not our job to judge others (e.g., our spouse, friends or pastors) or to reveal truth to them. Our job is to love them. The Holy Spirit is their teacher, as He is ours. If you discover that a friend or family member fails to understand important spiritual issues, pray for that person. You can trust God, who revealed the truth to you, to reveal it also to them—

in His time. Be gracious toward them. God will not judge them according to His revelation to you. He will judge them according to His revelation *to them*.

Don't feel compelled to *teach* them. Graciously offer this book to them and leave the matter to God. We can provide *information*, but only God can impart *revelation*! So be careful with whom you share issues like these. Careless conversation, especially when laced with pride and legalism, will totally destroy your spiritual credibility and possibly the relationship.

10. Never Accuse Others

Scripture calls Satan "the accuser of our brethren" (Revelation 12:10). When you accuse, blame or condemn others, you are being conformed to his image! If someone has failed spiritually, it's because Satan has deceived and defeated him or her in the matter. That person isn't the enemy. Never lose sight of who the true enemy of your soul is—Satan and all his demons.

11. Celebrate Every Victory

Pay attention to the victories you have in Christ. Magnify the Lord. How? Wildly celebrate what He does!

12. If Necessary, Continue the Battle

Continue to listen to the Lord for instructions. Some victories are instant; some are progressive. God didn't allow the children of Israel to take control of all the Promised Land at once. He told them He would give them the land on which they placed their feet. He gave it to them a little at a time so that they could learn to manage their newfound freedom (see Exodus 23:30).

If the warfare continues, it's likely a sign that either God is continuing to train you for an even larger assignment or that you've not yet identified, interpreted and dealt with the defilement correctly. After all, there's more than your life and family at stake here. There are nations hanging in the balance. Be faithful and watch for God's promotion!

Father, we pray for our readers.
Grant them revelation of both
Your truth and the enemy's lies.
Reveal to them anything among
their possessions that grieves Your Holy Spirit
and gives advantage to darkness.
Bless them with the discernment
and discipline to deal decisively with it.
Purify our hearts, our homes, our churches
and our businesses for Your name's sake.
Amen.

More Amazing Stories of Spiritual Housecleaning

More fascinating stories of spiritual housecleaning fill the following pages. Readers from around the world tell their testimonies of freedom from demonic strongholds that once brought oppression into their homes and lives. Be encouraged, and take time to reflect as you read each story. Let their experiences inspire you as you seek the Lord and carry out your own spiritual housecleaning projects.

Spiritual Terror in a Small Tennessee Town

It happened in the year 2003 in a small Tennessee town, where my family lived. We had never given much thought to spiritual warfare, until my family was attacked. Some close friends of ours had very recently dealt with the demonic possession of their 18-year-old son, who was into witchcraft. We were supporting them the best we could even though we were doubtful and afraid. This kind of thing just didn't happen in our experience, and we were not sure what to think about it.

Then things started to happen in our own home. My young children were frightened, even though we tried to protect them from knowing what was going on. We started to hear loud banging in the walls. My children and I suffered from demonic nightmares. On more than one occasion, my children and I were literally run out of our home by an unseen enemy. The demonic oppression that I felt was the worst feeling I have ever experienced in my life—I did not know that such a fear even existed. The only way I can describe it is that it was like an invisible wet blanket covering me, drenched in evil. My thoughts were slow, foggy and did not seem to be my own. I could not concentrate on anything anyone was saying to me.

The fear I felt was overwhelming and I had a constant sense of dread. I could not even bring myself to break through the suffocation to pray! Honestly, I was afraid to pray, afraid that I might provoke the evil to show itself in a way that would literally scare me to death—and afraid that the little faith I had would fail. It got bad enough that I would wake up to loud, evil chanting and could not discern if it was in my head or my actual bedroom. For a while I tried to ignore it. I would pretend it was not happening and that I was unafraid, but after suffering in utter fear for weeks, I finally turned to our previously mentioned friends and our pastor.

I was given a book to read called *Spiritual House Cleaning* written by Eddie and Alice Smith. It was the same book our friends had read while going through the horrifying ordeal with their son. I was amazed that what I read was right on the mark with what I was going through. I wasn't alone in this feeling! I wasn't crazy! Just reading the book scared me, and for days I could only get past the first few chapters, but when I finally got to the end, my eyes were open to the spiritual warfare going on around me. There were things right on the shelf with my Bible that should not have been there that I'd never given a second thought to! Although we never practiced any sort of witchcraft, we had such things as Tarot cards and runes. We had music and books that we should not have had. We even found a toy in my children's room that we had assumed said the Lord's Prayer correctly. Instead, it said "Our *mother* who art in heaven."

The pastor came and, with the help of our friends, we made a huge bonfire and burned everything that we would not have wanted Jesus to see if He were to show up at our home. It was almost exhilarating tossing our stuff into the pit. With every trip outside with something to burn, I felt more and more free. Our home felt cleaner. We were ashamed that we had so many things that defiled our home. We rebuked and bound Satan and his demons in the name of Jesus and then blessed our home. Immediately, the oppression lifted and my family was finally at ease in our home. I was no longer afraid to be in the house alone! I was no longer afraid to check on my kids in the middle of the night by myself!

Many in our church were doubtful and unsettled about what had gone on in our lives and home. After sharing our ordeal, some members actually left the church, not yet ready to deal with the fact that spiritual warfare is real and was going on in our quiet little town. Although I was sad, I could not blame them. I was of the same mind before it happened to my family. Still, our pastor was kept busy with the number of people in our church who decided to have a spiritual housecleaning of their own. Many went out and bought the book for themselves. Praise God!

We were brought closer to God and His truth, and I know that more eyes than mine were opened due to Eddie and Alice Smith. I learned what it really meant to prepare myself with the armor of God and that I should not be afraid.

To Eddie and Alice Smith, I cannot even begin to express my thanks. Keep teaching the truth to God's children and never stop glorifying the Lord.

Belinda Dawn Camp
Texas

Prayer Prevails Over a "Haunted House"

When I was eight years old (children are the enemy's easiest target), our family of seven lived in a very small, cramped house. My mother began to pray earnestly for a larger house. Looking through the ads in our local paper, she noticed an offer from another family to trade a large, old house for a smaller house. She fell in love with this house, built in 1910, a large two-story house in a quaint neighborhood. Amazingly enough, they traded houses with us for a small difference in price.

We were a family of Mennonite descent, a conservative Christian family, my parents very moral and intelligent—nothing strange about us. So when we began to notice strange things and tell our friends, they didn't doubt our veracity but really didn't believe what we observed.

As children we loved this house—with both a front and back set of stairs—to play hide and seek in. One night when my sister and I were left alone, we both heard a large crash overhead and what sounded like a strong wind blowing through the house. We ran upstairs to look but all the windows were closed, and nothing appeared amiss. This happened three times before we ran to the neighbor's house and he came back to our house with us. When my parents came home, the neighbor gave them a look and a wink and said, "They heard something."

I experienced terrible nightmares every night, but I accepted this as normal. I was terrified of the dark. There was a dark presence in the house that I could feel. This presence began to manifest itself to various members of the household, usually with the sound of heavy footsteps across the hall upstairs and then descending the back stairs. We heard doors slam and water running, and when we looked, the door was locked and no water was evident.

One time when our family went on vacation, two male friends house sat: One was an ex-motorcycle gang member and one was an ex-Marine who had served in Vietnam. When we arrived home from our vacation, they said they would never spend a night there again. They said that in the middle of the night they heard footsteps cross the hall, slowly descend the back stairs and come up to the door of the family room, and as they turned in bed, the steps turned around and went back up.

My father, an engineer, was entirely skeptical of the rest of us. One Sunday morning he had a bad migraine and stayed at home in bed while the rest of us went to church. About noon, he heard the side door slam and heard our voices and the sound of our sitting down around the dining-room table. When he went down to say "Hi," he found the doors locked and the house empty. We walked in a moment later and he was white as a sheet.

A humorous event happened one night as my mother was waiting up for my teenage brother to come home. As midnight approached, she heard the back door open and close and then the bathroom door close loudly. She walked over, and sure enough the door was locked and she pulled it with some force. Keeping an eye on the door, she walked back to the living room and whispered loudly, "Wally! Wally! There's an intruder." My father came down with his rifle, walked to the bathroom door and flung it open, and no one was there. My father was holding my crying mother with the rifle in his hand when my brother walked in and said, "I'll never be home late again!"

My worst experience was when I was a freshman in college. I came home one night to find the house dark, and my dog was barking and snarling at me, even baring his teeth. I made it past him and I could feel the usual fear descend on me as I busied myself and washed my hair in the kitchen sink. I heard a loud click, and I looked up to see the light cord swinging rapidly back and forth, as if someone had thrown it. Terrified,

I went back upstairs to my bedroom and switched on the radio loudly to drown out any sounds. Then I heard my mother call my name, so I switched it off, ran to the top of the stairs and yelled, "What?" relieved that someone was home, but I was met with silence. This happened three times. In desperation I called my girlfriend. The static on the line was so loud I had to yell. "What did you say? I can't hear you!" she yelled back. I finally hung up. Fortunately, my parents came home shortly after.

We had lived with these frightening experiences for nine years when we visited a family friend's church that he pastored. He said he didn't know why, but he felt impressed to preach from a passage in the Old Testament about having nothing to do with mediums, sorcerers, astrologers or witchcraft. Feeling certain that these noises we heard were demonic, we searched out a missionary from Brazil who told us to renounce it and cleanse our house in Jesus' name.

My father prayed throughout the house in Jesus' name, commanding the spirits of darkness to leave, and we noticed a very definite change. The house became silent, and that sense of fear lifted. My dreams became pleasant.

The family who had owned the house previous to us had a son who became a friend of my brother's. He later admitted, "We heard strange things all the time in that house." (That's why it was such a great bargain!) Yet those experiences taught me to identify the presence of evil and how to stand against it and prevail in prayer.

Connie Jost
Texas

The Death of a Drug Addict Tied to a Child's Insomnia

I was at a Freedom Ministry seminar where we had the opportunity to minister to 30 to 40 believers from Cook Island. During the lunch break, I had a conversation with a sister concerning her five-year-old son, Nicodemus, who had never slept in his room since they moved into their home a few years prior. My first prompting was to ask her if she knew about the concept of spiritual housecleaning and, to my surprise, she informed me that she just received your book *Spiritual House Cleaning*.

She and her husband asked me to take them through the application of the concepts described in your book, so we organized a night to carry out spiritual housecleaning in their home. When I arrived, I was warmly greeted by five-year-old Nicodemus, who was very fearful and still could not sleep in his room.

After a brief explanation of our action plan, we waited on the Lord and sought His guidance as we went through each room. When we entered the little boy's room (his parents and me only), I decided to turn out the lights and put out the challenge to them to ascertain what spiritual oppression they were experiencing. They were experiencing fear and darkness.

I was quite troubled in my spirit as I entered the room and eagerly waited on the voice of the Holy Spirit. My reply to the parents was that "a spirit of death is in this room" coupled with other spiritual forces such as suicide, rejection, fear and more, and that somebody had died in this room. The parents proceeded to inform me that neighbors told them years earlier that a drug-addicted young man died in this house.

Under the leadership of the Holy Spirit, we dealt with the spiritual forces, cleansed the room by applying, by faith, the precious blood of our Lord Jesus Christ, and then sanctified and dedicated the room to the Lord.

I also encouraged the parents to play some soft, anointed music at night and throughout the day to build up a spiritual atmosphere pleasing to the Lord in this room. To cut the story short, Nicodemus slept from this night forth in his own room.

All glory and praise to our Lord Jesus Christ!

Anonymous

Job Released as House Was Cleared

I was working in South Africa as a teacher. Since my husband did not get a work visa in South Africa, he had to go to the United Arab Emirates for a job. Soon I joined him and believed God for a job for myself.

All the time I was at home, I listened to tape recordings of Scriptures about faith. I knew my job was already given to me and I would thank

God every day. But months passed by without my getting a job. And then I asked the Lord, "Lord, I know Your promises are sure and it will always come to pass, but is there anything in my life that is hindering these promises from working well for me? If that's the case, please show me where the block is so that I can get rid of it and receive the promise You have given me."

By this time, I'd had some interviews but never got a call back from any of them. That's when I got a book by Derek Prince called *Blessing or Curse: You Can Choose!* Until that time, I had never heard about curses ruling a person's life. I thought that because Christ redeemed us from the curse of the Law, we could not have any curse coming into our lives. My dad used to tell me, as I put some decorative stuff in the house, that we shouldn't put these images in the house because it would bring a curse, but I never believed what he said.

Well, after I read this book, I fasted for three days, renouncing every curse in my life, confessing and renouncing things I had done, like going for yoga classes, going to the Hindu temple with my friends and indirectly worshiping their gods, taking their holy water, putting it on my head and all sorts of things I had done. The amazing fact was that the Holy Spirit reminded me about all those one by one—it just came flowing to my mind.

Then I searched my whole house and started throwing out rings that had demonic figures on them, silver "luck" chains, tapes, CDs, books and clothes with bad figures on them. I took a bag and threw it all out of the house. I even threw out carved images, thinking, "If there is any curse coming into our home through these figures, I might as well do without them." I didn't even want to ask myself whether it was okay to keep this and throw that—whatever didn't give me peace, I threw out.

After I did this, I was sitting in my living room praying and thanking God. The moment I finished, my phone started ringing and I got three job offers at once—I had difficulty choosing the right one! Finally I chose one and started working. Within a month, I got the best job in the bank!

By doing this, I knew it was not a lack of faith that held back my blessings; it was a lack of knowledge that held back my blessings. As I allowed God to move in and teach me what to do and as I obeyed Him, everything changed. Now when I go to India (I am Indian), whenever

I try to buy some bed covers, I scrutinize the print, as all those traditional prints may have the face or figure of a Hindu god imprinted on it. I choose carefully the things that will enter my house. If there is anything that doesn't give me peace, I don't let it come into my house. I pray you will do the same.

Sheba Daniel

A Possessed Painting

Several years ago, a friend gave me a painting as a going-away gift. My friend's husband had painted the picture, so it was very special. This young man loved to read about and study the spiritual things of the Indians. He had large collections of books and artifacts. Of course I took the painting, not realizing how it was going to open a door for demonic activity in my home. I put the painting away in a box until after our move to another town.

When we moved into our new home, and since my son liked Native American things, I decided to hang it on the wall in his room. About two months later, my son started talking in his sleep very loudly—something he had never done before. So my husband and I decided to pray over our home. For a while the sleep-talking stopped, but it wasn't very long afterward that not only was he talking but he also started sleepwalking. One night, he really gave us a scare when he unlocked his bedroom door that faced the backyard and ran around the house screaming. He finally ran to the front of the house and began banging on the front door, not knowing where he was. When my husband and I woke up, opened the front door and asked him how he got there, he said, "I don't know."

The following day, I went to his room and began to pray, asking the Lord what was in his room that was causing all these things to happen. I prayed again and I clearly heard God softly telling me to look at the Indian painting. This picture was of a warrior Indian on a horse. At the base, where the hoofs of the horse were, was a dead carcass of a buffalo and on the left thigh of the horse was a red handprint.

When I looked at the painting, in the holes where the eyes of the dead carcass used to be, I saw two demonic, peering eyes, red as the color of blood. An ugly, cold chill ran all over my body. I knew that I had to get rid of the painting. I asked the Lord what that was and He indicated to me that demons can possess anything and hide anywhere and go unnoticed for a long time. So I removed the painting from the wall and got rid of it. I prayed and anointed our home and my son had peace in his room. The demonic activity disappeared.

This is not to indicate that Indians are demonic or that the things they make are demonic, because I don't understand all the culture. I own some pictures of Indians and I love the Native American culture. I understand now that it's the spirit behind it that is empowering evil and creating fear. It's what we believe in. The young man who painted the picture, like us, didn't understand spiritual contracts of darkness, or he had an open door in his life that activated the demonic realm through his art. Praise God we are free regardless.

Thank you,

Mary Martinez
Texas

A Church Reborn in Washington, D.C.

Rats fleeing the building or staring you down at your doorway. Roaches filling the hallway, crunching underfoot. Huge black crows lined up on your fence, squawking at you. Sounds like a scene from a horror flick when the viewing audience wants to scream, "No! Don't go in there!" Many may have been saying just that. But the grace of God kept us here.

We were ministers in West Virginia at a large Baptist church when we were offered the opportunity to come to Washington, D.C. to "restart" a Baptist church that had, in 1996, suspended its constitution. This once-thriving church had fallen into disrepair as the congregation aged and dwindled down to a handful of elderly folks.

Two statements sum it up best: (1) *We knew about the blessings of God but knew little about the activity of the enemy*, and (2) *We didn't have a testimony until we came here*. When you are doing very little to oppose the enemy, there's little opposition from him. When we accepted this assignment, basically, to help this church, we declared war.

Before our start date of April 1, 1997, our former prayer pastor, Marty Cassidy, told us we needed to attend a spiritual warfare conference in Virginia Beach. This became the foundation that sustained us through the toughest times. We made connections with prayer warriors and mentors who would speak into our lives, pray for us, impart Holy Spirit wisdom and, at times, refuse to confirm what we thought was the Lord calling us out of D.C. In fact, we couldn't get agreement from anyone on that. So we stuck it out.

Although spiritual mapping was new to us, we started to understand that we were a gateway into the city. We are still getting revelation on the importance of our location—the northwest entrance into the nation's capital. We also began to see why the enemy wanted to kill the church and keep it dead. Our spiritual housecleaning became deliberate and desperate. Prayer was focused in our sanctuary, which was unusable and in disrepair. We anointed the church and prayed over it, section by section.

We immediately saw dramatic results. The next day, dead cockroaches filled the hallways. Exterminators were parked throughout the neighborhood, reporting that the rats seemed to be fleeing from the church. Note that the Holy Spirit was the only exterminator we had invited into the facility! Another time, a rat was sitting on our porch staring at our doorway. Even yelling and stomping didn't move him. We prayed God's blessings over the church and, after we left for a few minutes to go get a witness, the rat was gone. Rodent terrorists!

We exterminated many things. We researched church minutes from past business meetings, consultants' reports, library documents, anything to shed light and uncover darkness in the church's past. In the church hallway, former pastors' portraits chronicled the church history. We studied each one: this pastor fell into sin; that one died in a plane crash; this one misspent thousands of dollars. We decided to take down all the pictures.

Fast forward to the year 2000. We hosted the Glory Fire Conference for Mike and Cindy Jacobs. When Chuck Pierce came into the pastor's office, he remarked that he couldn't pray in there—it was too dark. Chuck recalled that he had smuggled Bibles into Russia and that it was a dark region of the world, but he said our church was the darkest place he had ever been.

Logic didn't rule our actions—we surrendered our reason to the Holy Spirit and operated on raw spiritual instinct. We thought the house behind the church should be ours, so we prayed for it for three years. It was the oldest house in Chevy Chase, Maryland, a very dark, Addams Family-like house. But because God doesn't have to be logical either, He got us the house.

After a dramatic exterior renovation, we unknowingly invited a flock of *huge* crows to our property. They daily objected to our presence. Most birds fly away as you approach—these birds looked at us in defiance, squawking aggressively as we passed. They perched atop the fence that we had to pass to get out the gate into the back of the church. We were "not in Kansas anymore" but felt the same torment that the scarecrow in Oz felt! Two interesting things about crows: (1) To "eat crow" means to retract a statement or admit an error (something we were unwilling to do); and (2) a group of crows is referred to as "a murder of crows" (enough said). We started rebuking the crows. They stopped coming and we haven't seen one since.

The warfare continues, but the spiritual housecleaning certainly lessened the physical manifestations. While much of our focus was to get rid of the bad stuff, we also made an effort to give away the good stuff. Pride and selfishness reigned in the former church, so we tried to operate in the opposite spirit. Our facility was crammed with pianos, furniture, pool tables, organs and other valuable "stuff." So we called around and gave it away to struggling churches in the area. When gutting our chapel, the pews went to a new Haitian church. Their members had been bringing in their own kitchen chairs each Sunday. How amazing is God?

So where do we stand today? We have opened our doors to many ministries with a desire to be a part of Kingdom work. Our congregation is multiethnic and international, and we minister alongside Korean, Burmese, Panamanian, French African and Ethiopian ministries. We have also been home to Ghanaian, Brazilian, Gypsy and Kenyan congregations that have gone on to larger facilities. Many times, people visiting the city join us for Spirit-led, prophetic worship and then ask if there is a "more Baptist church" nearby. We are always gracious to lead them to one they might find more comfortable. We take our role as gatekeepers very seriously.

We praise God that He has always provided praying people to stand as watchmen with us. We have enormous faith that He who began a good work will be faithful to complete it.

Rev. David and Rev. Maureen Freshour
Washington, D.C.

Cleansing a House of Witchcraft

We were so excited when we finally started looking at houses to buy, as our home is ministry headquarters. (No wonder the enemy attacks it and seeks to infiltrate it!) We had been asking the Lord for the right timing and to find us a house where He wanted us to minister.

When we finally found the house, I was somewhat apprehensive. It might have had something to do with a dream I had about the house. After visiting this house, I dreamed of a snake on one of the cabinets in the kitchen. I wasn't afraid, just upset, and in the dream I was asking the Lord what it meant. Then I saw a rainbow cover the back of the snake and I heard the Lord say, "I am giving you this house, but you will have to fight for it (not unlike the Promised Land)." So we went forward and the Lord kept opening one door after another.

Soon after we moved in, we had our pastor and his wife over. Together we prayed and dedicated our home to the Lord for His service. As we sat praying, I began to have a sense something was spiritually wrong in the house. Instead of disrupting the intention of our gathering, I felt like the Lord said to be patient, that He would uncover everything in His timing. So we dedicated the home and ourselves to Him for all He desired. (We sometimes feel, when we rent or purchase a property that we later discover is defiled, that we've missed God and made a mistake. We don't understand that God is reconciling all things to Himself. He often moves us into a property, onto a land, to take it back for His kingdom!)

Having been taught spiritual housecleaning early in our walk, we learned to discern the atmosphere in our home, but this was another level for us. The Lord revealed that there were high levels of witchcraft that had taken place in our home. I wasn't sure until we visited our neighbors and three different neighbors told us about the people who had lived there.

This was significant, because Scripture teaches that things are to be established by two or three witnesses (see Matthew 18:16). Our two closest neighbors told of how they were proclaimed witches and did sacrifices in the backyard. We even met the neighbor behind us who confirmed that a witch coven met between my house and their house. Their landlord was planning to tear down that house because of all of the decaying animal bones that brought termites. This would also explain why, when my dog was out in the yard, she would bring in bones.

We attended a deliverance conference for a week, where we were told that we were now clean and that we should go home to clean our house. We decided to wait until the whole family was together (spiritual housecleaning is a family affair). We put on praise music and had our three daughters read the Word out loud and worship while we went from room to room, asking the Lord to bring revelation of anything unpleasing that we—and the previous owners—had brought into the house. We asked the Lord about cleaning it deeper than just our stuff. We went through the whole house, top to bottom. We repented on behalf of the previous owners (identificational repentance) and took authority in Jesus' name, asking the Lord to remove every defiled thing and to apply the precious blood of the Lord Jesus Christ in its place (see Nehemiah 1:4-7; Psalm 106:4-8).

Since that time, we have become even more sensitive to the spiritual atmosphere in our house. When we share our testimony of victory, we are often asked to come and clean out others' homes. If the Lord allows us to go, we use it as a tool to teach them what God taught us about how to maintain the spiritual atmosphere in our home.

April
Ohio

In Closing

In Matthew 12:43-45, Jesus said, "When an unclean spirit goes out of a man, he goes through dry places, seeking rest, and finds none. Then he says, 'I will return to my house from which I came.' And when he comes, he finds it empty, swept, and put in order. Then he goes and takes with him seven other spirits more wicked than himself, and they enter and dwell there; and the last state of that man is worse than the first. So shall it also be with this wicked generation."

What do these verses tell us about the power and persistence of the demonic? Does it mean that if you do your spiritual housecleaning, several more spirits will come back and attack you? No, but the devil doesn't often give up ground easily. Take the example of when he tempted Jesus in the wilderness (see Matthew 4:1-11), attempting not once or twice but *three times* to get the Son of God to sin. But what is required to keep the atmosphere of your home spiritually clean?

Take some time to examine the spiritual environment in and around your home. Pray and ask the Holy Spirit to reveal anything to you that is offensive to God and disruptive to your home (taking a day or more to pray and fast is a good idea). Then, take note of what God shows you and of what He says to do. If necessary, call in your pastor or another mature believer to help you pray through your home and rid it of any defiled objects. Find favorite Scriptures to declare over your home, and then bless and dedicate it as a place of worship, peace, love and holiness—a place where God alone has total authority. It's often said that knowledge is power. However, that's not true. *Action* is power! Knowing what you've learned is step one. Taking action is step two. Now step out and do spiritual housecleaning!

Group Leader's Discussion Guide

For Small-Group or Congregational Teaching

This book is comprised of seven chapters that build one on top of the other. It is an excellent text for a spiritual warfare Bible study, a small-group study or a Sunday School quarterly.

We suggest that you teach the major points of each chapter from the text of each chapter. In advance, assign the Scripture references and stories contained in each lesson to different readers in the class. Encourage the class to read each chapter and to come with their answers to the questions. For chapters without questions, either create questions on your own or invite questions and/or discussions after the teaching portion.

Teach the major points, having students read the related Scriptures and testimonial stories as you come to them. Then allow students to share and discuss their answers to the questions that are part of the chapter. Their answers and experiences will likely spawn other questions and even more lively discussion.

With an engaged group, you should have a wonderful time of investigation and insight. Also, as students return in the subsequent weeks, they will begin sharing their breakthroughs as they experience the spiritual cleaning of their own homes and businesses.

(Note: Before engaging in church cleaning issues, be certain that you sit down with the pastoral team and submit your ideas and conclusions to them.)

Recommended Resources

Jackson, John Paul. *Buying and Selling the Souls of Our Children, A Closer Look at Pokemon*. N. Sutton, NH: Streams Publications, 2000.

Jacobs, Cindy. *Deliver Us from Evil*. Ventura, CA: Regal Books, 2001.

Pierce, Chuck. *Protecting Your Home from Spiritual Darkness*. Ventura. CA: Regal Books, 2004.

Prince, Derek. *They Shall Expel Demons*. Grand Rapids, MI: Chosen Books, 1998.

Smith, Alice. *Beyond the Lie: Finding Freedom from the Past*. Minneapolis, MN: Bethany House Publishers, 2006.

_____. *Delivering the Captives: Understanding the Strongman—and How to Defeat Him*. Minneapolis, MN. 2006.

_____. *Discerning the Climate of the City*. Houston, TX: SpiriTruth Publishing Co., 1997, (800) 569-4825.

_____. *Dispelling the Darkness*. Houston, TX: SpiriTruth Publishing Co. 1998, (800) 569-4825.

Smith, Eddie. *Breaking the Enemy's Grip*. Minneapolis, MN: Bethany House Publishers, 2004.

_____. *Strategic Prayer: Applying the Power of Targeted Prayer*. Minneapolis, MN: Bethany House Publishers, 2007.

Smith, Eddie and Alice. *Spiritual House Cleaning: Protect Your Home and Family from Spiritual Pollution*. Ventura, CA: Regal Books, 2003.

Wagner, Doris. *How to Minister Freedom*. Ventura, CA: Regal Books, 2005.

For all of Eddie and Alice Smith's books, CDs, DVDs or tapes, go to www.prayerbookstore.com

Additional Resources
from Eddie and Alice Smith

Eddie and Alice Smith, "America's Prayer Coaches," are best-selling authors and internationally known conference speakers. They teach together and individually on themes related to intercessory prayer, spiritual warfare and mapping, personal freedom and general discipleship.

Hosting the Smiths
For more information about the Smiths and how to host one or both of them for a conference in your church or city, go to www.eddieandalice.com

Prayer Resources
For Eddie's and Alice's books and materials, as well as other resources they recommend, go to www.prayerbookstore.com

Free Online School of Prayer
The Smiths offer a free online 52-week school of prayer at www.teachmetopray.com

Renewal Resources
Eddie and Alice offer a renewal resources site at www.windsoffire.com

Contact Information
Eddie and Alice Smith Ministries
U.S. Prayer Center
7710-T Cherry Park Dr., Ste. 224
Houston, TX 77095

Phone: (713) 466-4009
Toll-Free: (800) 569-4825
Fax: (713) 466-5633

Email: usprayercenter@cs.com

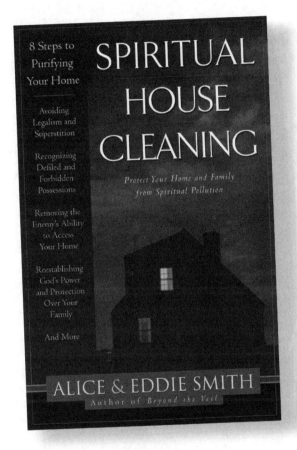